Judaism & Shintoism:

Possible Correlations Between Two Ancient Faiths

By Joseph A. Schiller

Judaism and Shintoism – Possible Correlations Between Two Ancient Faiths

By Joseph A. Schiller

ISBN 979-8-9860275-7-9

Printed in the United States of America

1st Edition – 1st Printing

Contributions
Editing: Nick Stead
Book Design and Layout: Morgan Guige

Publisher
Joseph A. Schiller
jaschiller1979@gmail.com
http://josephschiller.weebly.com/non-fiction.html
https://www.facebook.com/profile.php?id=100088864393074

For my parents, Bill and Sheila Schiller, for always en-
couraging me to raise the expectations I have for myself.

Table of Contents

Prologue

Like most young people growing up in the United States, with parents that wanted me to be raised in a denomination of Christianity, I was at least marginally familiar with the doctrinal and ritualistic trappings of that faith, and to a small degree that of Judaism as well. I was, however, unfamiliar at best with other world religions beyond the minimum academic requirements of grade school. This did not preclude me, though, from having a deep interest in them. After high school, I had the opportunity to live in Japan for a little more than a year. From the very day I arrived in Japan, I strove to learn as much as I could. While my survival instincts made learning the language a priority, I sought any and all knowledge I could about the history, customs, religious traditions, etc. of my temporary home. This was how I was first exposed to Shintoism. Shintoism, for the sake of oversimplification, and only meant as such, is the animistic or early set of spiritual beliefs of those on the archipelago nation prior to the introduction of Buddhism. It was from these amateur investigations that I first took notice of and became intensely interested in the various possible correlations between Judaism and Shintoism. I myself would never have suspected that there was potentially a whole range of reasons to investigate the connections between these spiritual heritages of two faiths with seemingly polar opposite perspectives. There were for me, however, numerous immediate and obvious observable similarities between Shintoism and Judaism which sparked a great interest in exploring further the nature of these correlations. Were these coincidental, or is there a very real link between these two faiths in the ancient past that has not yet been revealed?

This has been a project of passion for close to twenty-five years. It is precisely because there is not a greater understanding of Shintoism, and, therefore, an awareness of how this spiritual tradition is possibly connected to other faiths beyond the islands of Japan, that I chose to begin this scholarly journey. I feel that there is a tremendous amount more yet unknown about the true nature and story of ancient man. The mainstream academic community would rather ignore or not accept the evidence, or not enough evidence has been revealed and uncovered. Therefore, I do hope that this investigation and others like it will in some small way contribute positively to the overall body of historical and comparative religious studies.

Introduction

One should be forgiven for thinking it counterintuitive that there would be any significant correlations between the Jewish faith and that of Shintoism, or that of the ancient Israelites and Japanese for that matter. Isaiah Ben-Dosan stated it best: "Few peoples are as fundamen tally dissimilar as the Japanese and the Jews." Or at least appear to be. This may in a large part be due to the relatively little that most people know of Shintoism, its collective spiritual views or rituals, and, therefore, the inability to draw any immediate comparisons with Judaism as one may more easily do with Christianity or Islam, for example. Many people are traditionally raised, or at least those born with a predominantly Judea-Christian background are, with the understanding that Judaism is, based on its Semitic connections with the early proto-Judeo religious heritage of the Canaanites from which it is believed to have evolved, and due in part to the role and influence that Zoroastrianism played in the development of the practices and interpretation of doctrine thereof, directly tied to and an influence on other categorically Semitic belief systems to emerge later; again, such as Christia-

3

nity and Islam. Thus, many are, by default, conditioned to understand that Eastern Asian religious traditions are categorically and fundamentally different from those of Western Asia and elsewhere. It is arguable that, if a large percentage of people were polled to list the systems of faith in Eastern Asia, a strong portion could not or would not even list Shintoism.

This is perpetuated in part by the way in which scholars present information about religious traditions. One such example is in the very black and white nature often used for the categorization of this information. Most people are taught to understand religious belief systems to fall within one of two camps: monotheistic (belief in one deity) or polytheistic (worship of more than one deity). This very simplistic, and not altogether misleading, means of promoting the comparative understanding of spiritual traditions, more often than not, conditions people to instinctively assume there are little to no relationships between monotheistic or polytheistic faiths, for instance. The average consumer of information, can, therefore, be very easily drawn to a sense, unconsciously perhaps, that some spiritual perspectives have emerged independently of others. This subject area is much more nuanced than that. Take, for instance, the doctrine and principles associated with Jesus Christ. The Eastern Asian, Buddhist, and Hindu influences on the once divergent sect of Judaism now known ubiquitously as Christianity cannot be ignored. While most Christians want to believe that their faith is merely a continuation of the covenant between God and man as initiated between their god and Abraham, there is no question Christianity has a very Asian sub-context of flavor.

Another condition by which some may find themselves challenged to recognize any immediate relationship between Judaism and Shintoism is the cultural, linguistic, geographic, ethnographic, and historical differences between the Jewish and Japanese peoples, which on the surface seem to exist on opposite ends of a metaphorical spectrum from each other. Case in point, if a thousand random people from around the world were polled with the question, "What is historically the religious tradition of Japan?" the vast majority of those contributing would answer nearly unanimously with Buddhism. This is not to say that Buddhism is not a historical part of Japan's religious tradition, but it does not represent the full picture, especially in the ancient world, and is, therefore, not the religious tradition of Japan. This hypothetical example illustrates the idea that most people have a disproportionate religio-historical understanding of these two faiths. The observation that many do not associate Japan with any other set of spiritual traditions than Buddhism, and perhaps also, to a small degree, that some do not consider Shintoism a religion to begin with, but rather animism or a proto religion, contributes to an overall lack of necessary awareness on the subject. Additionally, most Western scholars have fallen into the trap of attempting to interpret unfamiliar spiritual traditions from their native Western lenses.

Relying on preconceived notions about religion, Western commentators have often molded their narratives of Shinto into a form convenient and digestible for their Western audience. Extrapolating from the religions in their own cultures, Westerners often look in other religions for a scriptural foundation and narratives about gods creating the world.

The same interpretive shortcoming also often befalls *Old Testament* scholarship as well.

Case in point, for hundreds of years it has been perpetuated that Christianity and Islam are text-based faiths, came out of the predecessor religious system, and another supposed text-based tradition, Judaism. Many scholars that oppose any Judeo-Shinto connections conversely identify Shintoism as being a faith devoid of such concrete doctrinal roots, and, therefore, fundamentally different foundationally. Arguably, Shintoism was not originally a strictly codified tradition, thus reflected in its early existential nature. The transformation to a more dogma-based faith does not take place until after the beginning of the Yayoi period and the beginning of the growing political, cultural, and social influences from the mainland.

The supposition, however, that Judaism is a text-based faith, and exclusively so, is, according to many, based on the argument that the *Torah* played, and continues to play, a central role in the faith. This conclusion, however, presupposes a couple of things. First, that those responsible for recording what are now the books of the *Torah* did so from a singular source, and the intention of having the *Torah* be the exclusive doctrinal genesis of the faith. And, secondly, that the *Torah* was, therefore, the only historical origin of doctrine for Judaism. Unfortunately, neither argument is accurate. The facts support a very different reality – that ancient Judaism, like Shintoism, was, before its own essentialist transformation during and post-Exile, originally existential in nature.

The written document containing the collective early

6

histories of the Jewish people, the *Torah*, was transcribed thousands and hundreds of years after the events,
circumstances, and stories they describe. In fact, most
scholars agree that the collected works that became the
Torah were compiled during and from texts written during the Exile and post-Exile periods. So, how then can
a book have been the basis of a faith retroactively? Well,
it cannot. The truth of the matter is that most early Jews
were not even aware of or taught from any unified body
of doctrine, probably lived their entire lives having no
more than a passing awareness of the supposed prophets
or their proclamations and were likely perfectly content
following their local brand of cult worship, however that
local cult worship may have aligned with the growing
popularity of Yahwism. To put it simply, the *Torah* has
no more of a relationship to Judaism's foundations than
the *Nihon Shoki* does with Shintoism, the *Amarna Tablets* with Babylonian spiritualism, or the *Book of the
Dead* with Egyptian religiosity, and, therefore, cannot
be the basis for arguing that Judaism, along with Zoroastrianism, were somehow the original traditions of
a unique line of religious belief systems fundamentally
and diametrically different from what emerged further
east across Asia.

For many, it is simply too difficult to accept that a civilization in Southwest Asia and one tens of thousands of
miles away in Far East Asia could have had any possible
connections whatsoever, no matter how significant, in
the ancient world. Scholars are redefining the historical
record every day, and part of that is the recognition that
the ancient world was a much more interconnected set of
realms than many have yet been willing to accept. Despite this academic progress, old mindsets linger. While

the frequency and speed at which communication and transportation of goods, ideas, and people between the varying groups in the ancient world could not resemble anything like what we see in our modern world, it did happen. It happened far more often, and it had a much more lasting impact than some would like to concede. Joseph M. Kitagawa, in his preface to Donald L. Philippi's *Norito*, defines this idea of "hermeneutical distance" best when he states:

> Sometimes, however, especially when we have firmly entrenched preconceived notions – for example, a certain political ideology, evolutionary dogma, or doctrinaire religious belief – our prejudgment becomes a stumbling block to understanding the text in question.

In any historical investigation the variety and strength of the evidence presented to support any conclusions, arguments, or suggestions is paramount. Nearly all of the evidence available for evaluation of the possible connections between Judaism and Shintoism is based either on text evidence, as is largely the case with Judaism, and observations, or oral traditions thereof, in the case primarily of Shintoism. Textual evidence, when based on ancient documents, only takes a researcher so far before other more substantial sources of information are needed to deepen the reliability of the study. One of the challenges inherent in this particular study, therefore, is that one cannot now make observations of ancient Shintoism's or Judaism's past, and what is observable of the modern iterations of both Judaism and Shintoism may not be, and are likely not, very close to the ancient or original forms. Some might use this reality as a way of justifying why they believe conclusions cannot be made about the nature of Judaism's potential roots in Shintoism. But the same could be said of the text evidence in this case as well, that of the *Old Testament* and ancient Japanese texts, the *Nihon Shoki* and *Kojiki*. If researchers can have faith in the Biblical and early Japanese textual accounts and use them as one might as textbooks from the ancient world of sorts, then those very same researchers can and should extend that very same faith to the eyewitness accounts that are available and any current observable correlations. The fact of the matter is that there are plenty of currently observable and recorded accounts made by eyewitnesses around the beginning of the Meiji era in Japan that correspond with the ancient written accounts to provide a proper basis for the conclusions and correlations outlined in this study.

Over the past several hundred years, the Western world (usually understood to be Western Europe, the United States, etc.) has dominated much of the global narrative, and that global narrative is very Judeo-Christian in nature; one of the legacies of the colonial era. This includes, for instance, the disproportionate emphasis placed on Judeo-Christian connections to the historical dialogue as promoted in grade schools and collegiate textbooks adopted and emphasized by a large portion of the world. It has only been within the last few decades that those revisionists seeking a more balanced, accurate, and inclusive conversation have been able to make considerable progress. It has also only been more recently that the religious studies departments at most colleges and universities, at least in the Western world, have become more inclusive of serious scholarship in other world religions, and willing to share the stage, so to speak, with them.

The West still produces a vast majority of historical scholarly literature available, however. And since an overwhelming portion of that work is printed or available only in English by authors and researchers that do not have command of foreign languages sufficient enough to include material in unfamiliar languages, there will inherently be a significant portion of the spectrum of scholarly research missing regarding certain spiritual realities. Again, Kitagawa states it best:

> It should be noted that the Japanology in question was a variation on what was usually called in the West a discipline that examined various facets of Eastern peoples – their languages, arts, economic systems, social and political orders, religions, and cultures – and yields "data" that were then subjected to scholarly analysis and interpretation based on "Western" models, concepts, and logic.

Unfortunately, I, as the author, while being able to communicate semi-fluently in conversation in Japanese, cannot read and write beyond a first or second-year grade school level, and therefore, cannot take advantage of any literature produced in Japanese unless it is first translated into English. This, of course, forces me to acknowledge that there may be perceptions, facts, observations, or otherwise, which could or should influence the work upon which I am engaged but sadly will not.

A generally comparative study of two or more belief systems, the relationships or lack thereof between them, and the evaluation of the various characteristics by which those faiths are or are not similar, is already difficult enough. When drawing comparisons between Shintoism and Judaism, and for the reasons previously outlined, as well as perhaps others, there are a set of unique challenges. Nevertheless, and while I may not be able to mitigate all of these academic hurdles, perhaps I may be able to drive the conversation forward a little more concerning the possibly relevant relationship between Judaism and Shintoism.

Chapter 1
Origins of a Theory

T he general set of understandings about the possible relationship between the Ten Lost Tribes of Israel and the ancient Japanese people – both peoples who believe their homeland to be divinely given to them – are collectively known as the *Japanese-Jewish Common Ancestry Theory*, or *Nichiyu Dousoron* as it is referred to in Japanese. These are the collection of suggestions that there are genetic, religious, and customary linkages that ultimately prove that the Japanese people, in part, are descended from the Lost Ten Tribes of Israel. Some versions proposed of the theory argue for an overall connection between the Lost Tribes and the nation of Japan as a whole, while others suggest that a few groups or tribes in Japan are descendants. As early as the sixteenth century, and the beginnings of Western or European contact directly with Asia, missionaries, merchants, and explorers began to express what they believed and recognized as similarities between various Asian peoples and Judaism, or the Lost Tribes of Israel.

A more fully developed set of ideas was first proposed

by a Scotch missionary living in Japan in the 1870s, Nicholas McLeod (also believed to be Norman McLeod in some sources). It must be noted that McLeod was not a trained historian or scholar, and only had a marginal command of Japanese, and, therefore, most of his conclusions came from conversations and observations. Nearly all of his conclusions can be dismissed outright as mere fantasy, owing to the fact that they cannot be supported by any discoverable facts or evidence. For example, McLeod states that the Japanese race is the Biblical fulfillment of the curse on Noah's son Ham, and blessings on his other sons Shem and Japhet. While much of what he argues can be ignored, McLeod does, however, outline several points about the noticeable similarities between the Japanese and ancient Israelites that are worth further, and serious, exploration from a more objective perspective.

One of the many theories identified by McLeod was that some tribes of Japanese were descended from Jews that migrated eastward and eventually crossed into Japan from China or Korea. The first major Japanese academic to delve into and continue work on this theory was Saeki Yoshiro, a professor at Japan's prestigious Waseda University, in the early 1900s. According to Saeki, who was supposedly an expert on Japanese Nestorianism, several Japanese tribes, such as the Hata, Hojo, or Taira clans, were Nestorian Jews that made their way into Japan from Korea in the third century CE. Saeki's work expanded on the idea that there may be some genetic linkage between at least some Japanese with Jewish communities elsewhere. Some believe this transition in Japan took place when the Yayoi culture displaced the Joumon culture as the dominant group on the main islands (see Chapter 11 for further discussion). Japanese scholars of the Meiji period seem to have gravitated toward the investigation of this possible connection. Dr. Jenichiro Oyabe, a graduate of Yale University, promoted a book he published in the 1920's with many of the same conclusions, even gaining audience with the royal family regarding the subject. Unfortunately, the author of this study found getting a copy of this book for reference was impossible in any form.

Both McLeod and Saeki were criticized early on and still are. McLeod, for his part, has been accused of promoting a religious connection between the Judeo-Christian world and Asia as part of some kind of spiritual support for Western imperialism in Asia, and of the overall growing Christian Zionism of that time. Some have gone as far as to say that the Japanese-Jewish Common Ancestry Theory was popularized by men such as McLeod for the purpose of arguing for the inferiority of the ethnic Asian races, and the superiority of the white, Judeo-Christian world. At the same time, the common ancestry theory of the Jews and the Japanese is not the only such proposed connection. The fact is clearly made by David Goodman and Masanori Miyazawa that many marginalized peoples throughout history have used such argumentation as the ideological basis for rejecting European Christian colonialism.

Nevertheless, as it is impossible to know the true personal, racial, spiritual, or geopolitical opinions that support the theories outlined with the Japanese-Jewish Common Ancestry Theory (except for where they were made explicit), the writings of McLeod, *Epitome of the Ancient History of Japan*, first published while in Japan and again after returning home, did nothing more than make an attempt to study the possible correlations between the Japanese people and the Israelites. It also seems highly unlikely that a Japanese scholar such as Saeki would have dedicated themselves to studying the Japanese-Jewish connection if there was an understood inferior imperial, racial, or other ulterior theme to the subject. The overall influence Judaism and those identifying as Jews have had in Japan is non-existent at best. At any given time in recent history, there have only ever been a few hundred people that have self-identified as practicing Jews, and of those nearly all were foreign nationals residing for one reason or another in Japan. It seems highly improbable that there has ever been a powerful enough tug on the Japanese psyche to suggest bias in the motivations for Japanese scholars wanting to study this topic. It is, however, possible that McLeod was in some way a victim of the popular Zionist fervor popular in his day among the British Empire (and elsewhere) and was unaware of the influence thereof.

Irrespective of any shortcomings McLeod himself or his attempted research had, or any influences he may have been subject to, the author believes informal researchers like him, and other academics such as Saeki, were genuinely trying to make sense of characteristics between the Judeo-Christian world and the similarities found in Japan and with the practices of Shintoism and were not consciously trying to steer the conclusions based on any ulterior motives. The fact of the matter is that the collective evidence can speak for itself and does not require any assistance in doing so.

Chapter 2
A Lost Tribe of Israel?

The Israelites, one of the names by which the Jewish people refer to the body of the faithful (the term "Jew" originally referred to those from the Southern Kingdom of Judah, but later became more universally used for all children of the covenant), was the name taken by, initially, the extended families of descendants from the land of Canaan in supposed captivity in Egypt, named after their founding patriarch Jacob, whose name was, according to the Biblical story, changed by God to Israel upon joining into a covenant with God. Also based on the traditions outlined in the *Old Testament*, the descendants of the twelve sons of Israel (Reuben, Simeon, Levi, Judah, Zebulon, Issachar, Dan, Gad, Asher, Naphtali, Joseph, and Benjamin) became the foundation of the Twelve Tribes of Israel that later, in their telling, returned to their promised land in Canaan. The House of Levi did not inherit land in the new Kingdom of Israel since it was the tribe of priests. However, Joseph's two sons, Ephraim and Manasseh, were bestowed with the eleventh and twelfth portions of the inheritance of land.

About two hundred years after the death of King Solomon, which is accepted to have been in the tenth century BCE, and believed to have been the end of the greatest period of the Kingdom of Israel, the kingdom began experiencing political turmoil which resulted in the splitting of the realm into two, the Northern Kingdom of Israel (Reuben, Gad, Ephraim, Issachar, Zebulon, Naphtali, Asher, Simeon, and Manasseh) and the Southern Kingdom of Judea (Judah, Simeon, and Benjamin). Beginning in the eighth century BCE, the tribes of the Northern Kingdom were gradually conquered by Assyria and forced into exile (including some of the tribes of Judah, Simeon, and Benjamin). Most of these ten tribes were, according to the story, forced to leave their homeland and resettle throughout the Assyrian Empire. According to Josephus Flavius, the first century CE Roman historian, this took place around the year 722 BCE. Unfortunately, only two verses of the *Bible* are dedicated to this. Additionally, some were exiled by way of Egypt to Kush, in what is now southern Egypt and the Sudan (Isaiah 11:11), and possibly in parts of what is now Ethiopia. The descendants of these twelve tribes began to be subsequently referred to as the Lost Ten Tribes of Israel, even after some of those descendants found their way back to Israel – when later living under Babylonian rule, they were allowed to return. A couple of centuries after the initial Exile initiated by the Assyrian invasion, the Babylonians, who displaced the Assyrians as the dominant political force in the Southwest Asian region, exiled the remaining tribes in the Northern Kingdom. They were settled further in the northern districts of that land.

The exacting details of the history of the Exiles, while important, do not need to be outlined in any tremendous

details for this study. For those that do want a more thorough scholarship on the subject, and a much more detailed investigation thereof, I recommend Prof. Avidgor
Shachan's book *In the Footsteps of the Lost Ten Tribes.*

The Lost Tribes of Israel

Not all of the descendants of the Lost Tribes of Israel
chose to migrate back to the land of Israel, or *Eretz Israel*.
Many remained in the lands of Assyria/Babylon where
they were resettled according to the *Bible*; specifically,
the lands of Chalach (modern Iraq), the Medes (in northern Iraq and northwest Iran), modern-day Kurdistan,
and Chavor (modern-day Syria). It is, however, possible,
as will be mentioned later, that the land of Chalach is
Khallakh in northeast Afghanistan, and Chavor is Khyber. Still, many others are believed, in part because of the
stories of the *Bible*, and in part from traditions passed
down by other groups of people in Asia, to have traveled
and settled even further away to the Far East.

The *Old Testament* gives very little in the way of detail
on this subject. The only other reliable early source is a
passage by Josephus Flavius in his work, *The Antiquities
of the Jews*, in which the author states that many of the
descendants of the Lost Tribes of Israel settled beyond
the Euphrates. While Josephus is generally considered
a trustworthy and credible source from the age in which
he lived, it must be noted that his comments about the
location of the Lost Tribes of Israel do come almost eight
centuries after the scattering of those tribes supposedly
took place, and, therefore, can only be considered hear-
say. There are, however, traditions told of the children of
Israel eventually settling in various parts of Asia, including Persia, Afghanistan, Pakistan, India, Southeast Asia,

China, Japan, etc. Other stories suggest groups of Israelites may have ventured into parts of Africa, Polynesia, and even the Americas. Researchers and scholars of various stripes have for hundreds of years tried to uncover where these Lost Tribes of Israel may have ultimately settled.

One popular theory is that some of the Israelites, instead of staying in Assyria, pushed further eastward, perhaps first settling in parts of Persia, and gradually making it all the way along the Silk Roads into Northern India, China, Myanmar, and Japan.

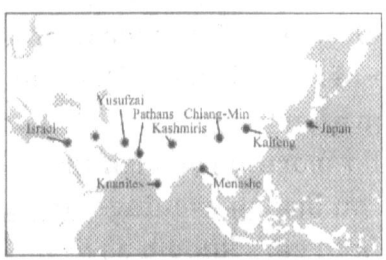

Fig. 1

Lost Tribes in Afghanistan

In what is now the modern nation-state of Afghanistan there are several tribal groups that maintain that their lineage stretches back to the Lost Tribes of Israel. More specifically, these people claim that they descend from the tribes of Ephraim and Manasseh. The name Yusuf, which means Joseph, is carried by many of these tribes, such as Yusufzai (Children of Joseph), Yusufuzi, and Yusufzad. These groups further proclaim that they are *Bani-Israel*, or children of Israel, and that they were once forced to leave their homeland. The *Old Testament* mentions that some of the Lost Tribes, in one of the very rare references to them after the Exile, migrated to "Halah and Habor" to the Far East. Joseph Eidelberg, one of several prominent scholars on this subject, mentions that the Hebrew pronunciation of these names is very similar to Khallakh and Khabor. Khallakh is an ancient city southwest of Issyk-kul (modern-day Kyrgyzstan) and the Khyber Mountains. Could the location at which some of the Lost Tribes of Israel settled be this area of northeastern Afghanistan?

To this day, many of these communities choose to remain isolated from the others. While these people are technically Muslim, they have several characteristic practices that are both unique and peculiar to them, and not based on their Islamic heritage in any way. These so-called Children of Joseph have Hebrew names, passed down generation after generation. They wear the fringes only traditionally worn by Jewish priests, light candles for the Sabbath on Friday evenings, and grow the curled hair in front of both ears known as *peyot* (side curls).

The Pathans

In modern Afghanistan, Pakistan, Iran, and India there is an ethnic group known as the Pathans, which has a traditional belief that they are descendants of the Lost Tribes of Israel. While they too, like many of those regions, are primarily devout Muslims, there are several practices and customs of theirs that are distinctively non-Islamic. Rather, they closely resemble Jewish customs.

For both Muslims and Jews alike, circumcision of males is one of the most important sacraments performed. But, for the Pathans, this ceremony is performed on the eighth day after birth as is done in Judaism, not on the twelfth birthday as in Islam. The Pathans have a traditional garb known as *kafan*, a garment with four corners that are tied together with strings, very reminiscent of the *tzitzit* in Judaism – something worn by Jews to distinguish themselves as children of Israel. On the Sabbath the Pathans bake twelve loaves of *hallah* (Jewish bread) while also lighting a candle and covering it with a breadbasket. The candle must be lit by a woman past menopause, as in Judaism. The *kosher* dietary laws followed by the Pathans are also closer to those of Jews than they are of their Muslim brothers and sisters. Horse and camel meat, not forbidden for Muslims, are acceptable for the Pathans.

Some of the elders of the Pathans still wear a small box called a *tefillin* (phylactery) containing a verse from the book of Deuteronomy 6:4. Again, a custom with no precedent in Islam. Like several tribal groups elsewhere in Afghanistan, mentioned above, the Pathans retain a number of family names of the Lost Tribes of Israel, such as Asher, Gad, Reuben, Naphtali, Ephraim, Manasseh, and other names that are not traditionally found in Islamic communities, i.e., Samael, Israel, etc. Also, like the Yusufzai tribesmen and tribeswomen, the Pathans refer to themselves as part of *Bani-Israel*. Along with having a general sense of being part of the heritage of remnants of the tribes of Israel, the Pathans honor the Tavrad El Sharif (the Torah of Moses) and show special reverence for the prophet Moses. Even the oral traditions of the Pathans reference how their tribal names are evolved forms of their corresponding tribe of Israel, such as the Rabbani tribe for Reuben, the Lewani tribe for Levi, the Ashuri tribe for Asher, and so on.

Lost Tribes in India

Eastward from Afghanistan in what is now Northern India, we find Kashmir. Place names, tribal names, and names of men and women have a long tradition of being strangely similar to Hebrew names. The tribe of Asheriya is Asher, the tribe of Gadha is Gad, the tribe of Lavi is Levi, and so on. In addition to tribal groups seemingly sharing qualities of names of the Lost Tribes of Israel, there are dozens of places in the Kashmir region that closely resemble names of the ancient Kingdom of Israel, such as Samaryah (Samaria), Mamre (Mamre), Pishgah (Pisgah), Heshba (Heshbon), Gochan (Gozen), and so on.

Many historians of the Kashmir peoples and the region maintain that the Kashmir tribes were the descendants of the Lost Tribes of Israel, as the priest Kitro did in his work *The General History of the Mughal Empire*, and the priest Monstrat did at the time of Vasco da Gama in the fifteenth century. There is one group in particular called the Yusmarg (think Yusuf) which calls itself B'nei Israel (Children of Israel), and it is said by many from the region that this is the ancient name of the people of Kashmir. The two most prominent historians of the Kashmir people, Mullas Nadiri (*The History of Kashmir*) and Ahmad (*Events of Kashmir*), both claim as fact in their respective works that the people of Kashmir originate from the Kingdom of Israel. There is also a folktale from the region which tells the story of Jesus, after His resurrection, traveling to find and visit the scattered peoples of the Lost Tribes, and spending time in Kashmir.

In addition to the speculations surrounding the Kashmir tribes, there is another group of people, the Knanites, which show signs of being connected in some way with the Lost Tribes of Israel. Knanite means, in the dialect of

Aramaic spoken by the people, "The People of Canaan," and these people to this day worship from the *Aramaic Bible*.

Lost Tribes in Myanmar

Along the border between the modern countries of India, China, and Myanmar lives a tribal group called the Menashe. The Menashe people actually refer to themselves as the Lusi ("Lu" means tribe and "si" means ten in the local Chinese dialect they speak).

Rabbi Eliyahu Avichail, the founder and one-time president of Amishav, an organization that seeks out the Ten Lost Tribes of Israel, traveled to and investigated the claims of the connection these people have made. On his visit, he learned that the people of the Menashe, when they pray, say, "Oh, God of Menashe," very similar to Manasseh, one of the Lost Tribes of Israel. There are numerous other tales that have survived among these people which describe a series of twists and turns from being exiled to Assyria, conquered by Babylon and later the Persians and Greeks, to being exiled to Afghanistan by the Persians, only to be conquered again by various Islamic kingdoms and forced to convert to Islam. Apparently, some of the Menashe made their way into Western China initially, and later Central China around the area of Kaifeng. According to these oral stories, the Chinese enslaved many of the Menashe, prompting a group of them to migrate into what is today Thailand and eventually Myanmar.

There is a traditional song still sung among the Menashe people with lyrics that come very close to the tale of the Exodus in the *Old Testament*.

> We must keep the Passover feast
> Because we crossed the Red Sea by dry land
> At night we crossed with a fire
> And by day with a cloud
> Enemies pursued us with chariots
> And the sea swallowed them up
> And used them as food for the fish
> And when we were thirsty
> We received water from the rock

Additionally, the name of the god of the Menashe is Y'wa, which of course is very close to that of the Hebrew god, *Yahweh*.

Among the Menashe communities, there is a tradition of having a priest that not only looks after the spiritual lives of the people but watches over them generally. These men are always called Aaron and wear a special tunic and breastplate resembling that described of the priests of the house of Levi. According to Rabbi Tokayer, an authority on this subject, the rituals he witnessed of the Menashe were straight out of the *Bible*. In fact, several thousand Menashe have made their way to Israel, migrating back to the Holy Land, as well as establishing synagogues in Myanmar as part of a general re-conversion to Judaism.

Lost Tribes in China

Further East along the Silk Roads we arrive in China. According to the writing of Rev. Thomas Torrance, in his 1937 book *China's First Missionaries: Ancient Israelites*, it was suggested that a small minority ethnic group called the Chiang were the descendants of the Israelites, part of the Lost Ten Tribes of Israel. Rev. Torrance's arguments stemmed from observations of these people he had made as a missionary.

While the evidence outlined by Torrance is not as extensive or even as strong as has been observed in other cultures, there were a couple of things that stood out to him worth noting. First, the Chiang people are monotheistic and are rare exceptions before the advent of Christianity in Asia. The god of the Chiang is called Yawei, which of course is similar to the Hebrew *Yahweh*. The priests of the Chiang wear all white and purify themselves when performing rituals, one of which is offering animals as a sacrifice to their god on an altar of uncut stones (similar to what is found in Exodus 20:25). The animals they sacrifice must undergo a similar process of purification. Unmarried men cannot become priests in their tradition (Leviticus 21:7, 13).

In addition to the Chiang people, there is a strong tradition that the city of Kaifeng has been connected to Judaism as far back as the first century CE. Joseph Eidelberg mentions that the tradition has Hebrews migrating into the Kaifeng area as early as about 205 BCE. There is nothing that stands out to suggest a connection with pre-Babylonian or post-Babylonian exile, however, some believe the long-standing relationship with the Holy Land, and the large numbers of Jews that have lived in the city for centuries may have something to do with a much earlier migration. The prophet Isaiah may have even referred to the lost tribes in China when he said, "Behold, these are coming from afar. These from the north and the west and from the land of Sinim." Sinim is, interestingly, the Hebrew name for China.

Lost Tribes in Japan

The big question left to the researcher now is, "Is there evidence that groups of Israelites, the Ten Lost Tribes of Israel, made their way further east, into Japan, perhaps?" Scholars already know that merchants from Israel were trading during the time of King Solomon across the Mediterranean basin, North and East Africa, and as far away as India. Therefore, it is not a stretch to be open-minded about the possibility that some of those tribes found their way, either along the Silk Roads across the land, or by way of the sea, as far as Japan. Could the name given to the land that some of the exiles eventually journeyed to, as possible with other parts of Asia, the Arzareth mentioned in the fourth book of Ezra, which according to some means "most far away land," be Japan?

Amishav

One of the single greatest collective efforts undertaken of serious research and investigations worldwide in search of possible remnants of the Lost Ten Tribes of Israel has been that of an organization known as Amishav. No study or exploration related in any way to the Lost Tribes of Israel can be considered without at least a cursory mention of the work conducted by Amishav. It should be mentioned that this scholarly investigatory undertaking does have a very practical purpose; that of verifying the validity of groups of people that claim to be of Jewish ancestry and who may be trying to seek residence in Israel based on that heritage. It is largely due to the tiresome work of the directors of Amishav, led by founder Rabbi Eliyahu Avichail, that so much is now known of many disparate peoples around the world that have verifiable Jewish ancestry, including most of those mentioned in this section, as mentioned earlier. Before he passed away, Rabbi Avichail and his team opened an investigation into the Jewish connection with Japan in 2007.

Chapter 3
Genetic Connections

N o evaluation of the possible correlations between the ancient Israelites and Judaism with the early Japanese and Shintoism could be considered complete without some analysis of the potential evidence for biological, or more precisely, genetic links between these two peoples. This is probably the most controversial of all the sub-theories of the Japanese-Jewish Common Ancestry Theory. Unlike the more subjective nature of the other sub-theories based more on observation, modern genetic science allows for, in theory, a much more objective means of study. It is upon this supposed objectivity that the controversy lies.

Nearly all genetic or biological arguments for the connection between the Japanese and ancient Israelites are based on studies done with Y-DNA (NRY), or the Y-chromosome of male DNA. Unlike females, who have two X chromosomes, males have one X and one Y chromosome. Chromosomes, X or Y, are made up of collections or groups of what are referred to as *haploid genotypes*, or *haplotypes*, each representing genes that are closely linked and inherited. In the case of Y-chromosomes, these inherited characteristics come from the father only. This is different from genotypes of mitochondrial DNA (mtD-NA) that are inherited from mothers only. In the case of the NRY, the *haplotypes* are passed on nearly unchanged from the father. The way in which the *haplotypes* can be studied is by comparing *haplotypes* between two or more groups of people. If a significant portion of the DNA is related, then it can be argued scientifically that there is a possible genetic linkage. The commonalities found genetically are called *haplogroups* and can be used to identify genetic linkages contemporarily and historically. The NRY has nineteen haplogroups (marked with the letters A to S), generally, though not entirely, based on geographic distinctions. The primary ancestor of all mankind has been labeled Y-chromosomal Adam.

The Japanese have a very characteristic feature on their NRY, referred to as the YAP gene sequence. It is unique because it is very rare among the neighboring Asian groups such as the Chinese and Koreans. This is important in the hunt for the genetic relationships between the Japanese and any other ethnicities because the YAP sequence is only found with haplogroups D and E. In other words, the YAP gene sequence is not connected to the other ethnic groups in East Asia. Haplogroups D and E, based on studies, at one point in the ancient Middle East were related to each other as DE but diverged. Therefore, one can use this genetic information to help screen for common ancestry, which would need to be part of haplogroup D or E and carry the YAP sequence. Nearly forty percent of the Japanese people's Y-DNA is of haplogroup D, fifty percent O (closely tied to Asian ethnicities), and ten percent other.

Haplogroup E, on the other hand, is found to make up about thirty percent of the Y-DNA of Jewish populations, such as the Ashkenazim, Sephardim, Djerba, in Kurdish-inhabited areas, Yemen, and the Samaritan Jews that never left the Holy Land. The haplogroup E also contains the rare YAP gene sequence. There is an ethnic group called the Chiang (see Chapter 2) that also carries a strong percentage of haplogroup D and the YAP sequence, which makes them a genetic relative of the Japanese. Some of the ethnic groups that are found to have both haplogroup E and the YAP gene sequence are the Pathans (see Chapter 2) of modern-day Afghanistan (see Chapter 2), Uzbek Jews, the Falasha (Ethiopian Jews), and the Igbo Jews from Nigeria (at an astounding 90%). These genetic connections give evidence supporting the various claims ethnic groups have of being part of the Lost Tribes of Israel as described in Chapter 2 and could be used to show where these groups migrated and settled.

What makes this part of the Japanese-Jewish Common Ancestry Theory so contentious are all of the traditional reasons why any broad genetic study is problematic. First of all, it must be mentioned that despite modern scientific and technological developments in the field of gene research, the field still lacks the precision that other areas of science have. Many of the conclusions, while accurate, are accurate within a range. Additionally, with respect to ancestral *haplogroup* relationships, applying proper dating becomes a challenge. There is not a consensus within the academic and/or scientific community about the adequate system of measuring the periods of noticeable mutations with *haplogroups*. Some people believe in the evolutionary theory model and timeline, while others prefer Carbon-14 dating, and there is a massive difference in the results obtained by each. According to evolution theorists the DE haplogroup split in the Middle East about fifty or sixty thousand years ago, whereas Carbon-14 dating places this event at several thousand years ago.

There is also a disagreement among scholars about which type of DNA study is most effective in analyzing not just contemporary genetics, but inherited relationships as well. Some believe the Y-chromosome studies do not produce results with the same levels of accuracy as mtDNA science can. Those that support mtDNA studies over NRY point to the fact that mtDNA results more accurately show genetic diversity. Consequently, those that disagree with the Japanese-Jewish Common Ancestry Theory use this, above almost all other sets of evidence, to try and prove their point. That argument is that there is much more genetic difference between the ancient Israelites and the Japanese as compared to what is found with NRY. It is true that mtDNA results are more solidly dependable. However, the accuracy of mtDNA studies is problematic in populations that were historically not relatively homogenous, and, therefore, mixed frequently, such as groups that were often migratory, or came into frequent contact with migratory people. If we are to take the *Old Testament* as relatively true in scope, then we know that there were several periods during which the Israelites were subjugated by other civilizations: the Egyptians, Assyrians, Babylonians, Persians, and as minorities across Europe, etc. Every time a Jewish female had a child with a gentile male, as a slave, servant, wife, or otherwise, that Israelite mtDNA was diluted permanently. Mitochondrial DNA results do a fabulous job of outlining the genetic mixing of a specific woman or group of women's pasts, but poorly show the broader *haplogroup* relationships. Therefore, I would argue that while mtDNA studies clearly have their place within the greater realm of genetic studies, longitudinal research on genetic groupings should remain based on NRY.

Another significant challenge with large-scale genetic studies lies in the fact that it is impossible for a group of people to be one hundred percent of any *haplogroup*. Groups of people, no matter how remote and isolated they may have been, still manage to mix with others and complicate the DNA signatures. The ancient Israelites, as is made clear from descriptions in the *Old Testament*, mixed with North African groups and later Asian ethnic groups. This means that a people that might have had ninety percent haplogroup DE would, over time, shed some of that homogeneity for a more blended DNA make-up. *Haplogroups* as a concept for aiding in genetic studies were created precisely because no group has avoided mixing over the thousands of centuries. The relationships between the *haplogroups*, however, provide the clues needed to identify ancestral relationships. As mentioned already, the common ancestral haplogroup for both D and E, along with the YAP gene sequence, was DE, from the region of Southwest Asia. The key to following the descendants of the ancient Israelites is thus to follow the YAP sequence through both the D and E haplogroups.

It may never be determined the exacting percentages of what a group now or in the ancient past had of certain DNA markers, but we can know which DNA *haplogroups* they carry, and how those groups were related in the past. If, for example, the only *haplogroups* with the YAP gene sequence were D & E, or DE in the ancient world, then any groups with DE, D, or E, along with the YAP sequence must be genetically related in some way. There is another possibility one must consider, and which will be explored in greater detail later. That is that the reason the Japanese people of today possess the D haplogroup and YAP gene sequence may not be because they are the descendants of the Lost Tribes of Israel, but instead because other migrant groups of Asiatic peoples from Siberia and elsewhere that moved into the islands of Japan mixed over the centuries with an already existing group on the islands that had these traits because they were in fact of Jewish heritage. Perhaps the Ainu peoples.

Chapter 4
Common Mythologies and Origin Stories

Pre-Judaism/Canaanite Religious Connections

Judaism is traditionally understood by the general public, and by the body of the faithful, to be, at least as it eventually evolved into, a monotheistic faith. The early form was, more accurately, however, a mono-lateral religion. Mono-lateral refers to the idea that while a religious tradition may worship, follow, or otherwise revere numerous deities, prominence and singular importance is given to one deity over all others. Shintoism is most frequently said to be polytheistic, due to the relationship of *kami* in the tradition. This, too, is entirely inaccurate. The fact is that Shintoism, too, is mono-lateral. While there are certainly thousands if not tens of thousands of *kami* recognized in Shintoism, it is believed that there is one all-powerful creative force that governs the heavens and earth – Ameno-minaka-nushi-no-kami.

What many scholars and members of the Jewish religious community fail to acknowledge, or are simply unaware of, is that the ancient Semitic peoples, the Canaanites, or synonymously the Phoenicians, among many others, were actually polytheistic before an evolution took place into initially mono-lateralism, and later monotheism. This may perhaps be because of certain phrases that are repeated throughout the *Old Testament* such as, "Thou shalt have no other gods before me." (Exodus 20:3). In reality, there are numerous references to the existence of multiple gods. Baal alone, which is the name used for a whole collection of deities, for example, is mentioned ninety times. In fact, a supposed competition between Yahweh and Baal was supposedly witnessed by a large number of people as described in part of the story about Elijah. According to the book of Second Kings, the goddess Asherah, the consort of El and/or Yahweh, was worshiped in the Temple until the prophet Josiah had the symbols of her cult removed from within. The very term used in the *Torah*, which has often been used synonymously with God, *elohim*, is actually "gods," and is therefore a plural noun. There are significant parallels between the understanding of *elohim* and *kami*.

> Until post-exilic times Yahwe was worshipped by Jews without any scruples together even with entirely strange gods in one and the same temple.

Regardless, the Israelites worshiped multiple gods alongside Yahweh. In addition to Asherah, the early Israelites worshiped Ashtaroth, Shamash, Yarekh, Molech, Dagon, Rahab, and various minor deities, collectively referred to in the *Torah* as Baal. In the early years of the proto nation of Israel, each tribe placed particular importance on one of the several deities of the Semitic pantheon, just as the neighboring peoples such as the Assyrians or Babylonians did. It should not be assumed that the cult of El and/or Yahweh was any more important for each of the twelve tribes of Israel as the local deities for which they built shrines and other such places of worship. To this point, nearly all of the cities of Canaan were known to have been the center of one of the cults among the pantheon; Jericho with Yarekh, Chemosh with Moab, Melqart with Tyre, and Yahweh with Jerusalem, for example. The growing political prominence of Jerusalem beginning with the period of kings is the first time that Yahweh not only gains its strongest foothold as a cult among the Israelites, but long-term will gradually win out as the only deity worshiped.

> "every Israelite member of a fully qualified *sib* (clan/extended family) originally had a shrine in his house and a house idol"

The god Yahweh does not first begin to gain singular prominence of place in the pantheon of Canaanite deities, though, until the supposed covenant he concludes with Abraham, and the demand of that commitment that Abraham makes to worship Yahweh, and only Yahweh. Even after Abraham agrees to solely worship El, or Yahweh (there is some ambiguity as to whether the god El and Yahweh were the same or if Yahweh displaced El in the Semitic pantheon), the Canaanite and later Israelite people often, and openly, worship the other deities of their culture. It should be noted that the Egyptian civilization also began undergoing a similar transformation from polytheism to monotheism/mono-lateralism before that civilization ultimately rejected the "new" tradition

36

of monotheism. If Egyptologists are to be believed, the brand of monotheism introduced to Egypt was, historically speaking, abruptly imposed or forced upon the nation, as opposed to a gradual rise to prominence as was among the Canaanites one generation at a time. It must be noted that the spiritual or religious reality of the land of Canaan was ever shifting and evolving alongside the shifting sands of religion in the more dominant civilizations in the region such as Egypt and throughout Mesopotamia. In fact, the Sabbath ritual was originally a full moon celebration for various versions of the moon deity of the Western Asian peoples before it was assimilated into the Yahwistic tradition, and it is only from the post-Exile period that it becomes such an important feature among the sacraments of Judaism.

The fact of the matter is that the long-term institutionalization of Yahweh as the singular and only acceptable figure of worship for the Israelites, the body of the faithful, came in the period after the exile of the Jews in Babylon. Much like the early efforts by the Catholic Church to settle on a uniform and consistent canon beginning with the Council of Nicaea, the remaining Jewish leadership in exile formalized the canon that is now, more or less, Judaism, and, therefore, the true beginnings of Jewish monotheism. Pre-Exile Judaism is thus more existentialist and becomes more essentialist post-exile (the same transformation took place with Shintoism between the period just before the Taika Era and continued thereafter). This means, of course, that any of those Lost Ten Tribes that did not settle in Babylon, or return to Israel when allowed to do so, were likely to have continued the more mono-lateral, a seemingly polytheistic, form of Judaism.

In addition to worshiping the various personifications of nature in the form of the pantheon of deities, the Semitic peoples of Western Asia, including the Canaanites and later early Israelites, practiced a form of ancestor worship, just as the Shinto faithful. Ancient Shintoism, as with ancient Judaism, would not have had any collective uniformity of a priesthood and/or the ecstatic practices thereof. While the body of spirituality across Israel, or Japan, would have shared a set of general cosmogenic and spiritual ideas and beliefs, each tribe or clan would have had their own distinct and unique variation of worship at shrines. This conformity of worship is never fully realized until the period of Exile and post-Exile.

There was also a strong tradition in Judaism of shrines and other holy sites being established upon hilltops and among sacred groves of trees just as is part of the practices in Shintoism. As Joseph Eidelberg states:

> In those days religion was simple. There were no priests, no temples, and no elaborate rituals. A tree, a grove, or a stone, were used as a sanctuary, and from there the Hebrew patriarchs maintained direct relations with the Lord.

Parallel Origin Stories

Using ancient mythologies as a basis for understanding the history of a people or place is problematic for several obvious reasons. References to dates or other forms of periodization are the most challenging. Many scholars, therefore, tend not to focus on the timeline of a myth, and, instead, focus on themes, names of people and places, and actions or deeds. Unfortunately, not every Biblical historian or theologian applies this caution when using the *Old and New Testaments*, and they place far too much trust in the texts, allowing in some cases for an almost literal understanding. The Book of Genesis, in particular, needs to be approached as just one historical artifact – like any other artifact – in order to more responsibly use it as such.

The case of early Japanese scripts such as the *Nihon Shoki* and *Kojiki* should not be exceptions to the principle. Like the stories of the *Bible*, the legends outlined in the *Nihon Shoki* and *Kojiki*, among other extant texts, began as oral traditions before they were ever committed to the page. It stands to reason that the tales would change from generation to generation, being retold with slight modifications, deletions, additions, and other alterations both purposeful and accidental. This would have been the case well before they were written down. Being recorded in hard form did not save these myths from the errors of man. Subsequent copies and translations of these texts would have had the same effect on them, only now with the added complications of incorrect interpretations, translations, and misunderstandings, all of which led and still lead to very different stories altogether. It is, therefore, important to keep in mind that while the books of the *Torah*, *Nihon Shoki*, and *Kojiki* are valuable resources for piecing together a picture of these cultures and peoples in the ancient past, one must be judicious with the interpretation of the reliability and accuracy of what is presented. This lens becomes particularly important for understanding the *Torah*, or first five books of the *Old Testament*, and the beginning portions of the *Nihon Shoki* and *Kojiki*.

Chapter 4

Genealogy

The genealogical origins of the Jewish peoples, at least according to the Biblical account, begin with Isaac, Abraham's son with his first wife Sarah, and his son Jacob, who supposedly tricked his father into blessing him with the birthright blessings that should have been due to his brother Esau. The story of Jacob continues with him later falling in love with Rachel, and his desire to make her his wife. According to Genesis, his father Isaac requires his son to seek Rachel's older sister's hand in marriage first before also asking to be wed to Rachel. According to the record passed down, Jacob reluctantly obeyed his father, and first wed the older sister, who he felt was ugly and displeased him, before then marrying Rachel.

Jacob would go on to have thirteen children with four wives, but it is said Rachel, his beloved, was barren for a long period. When she was finally able to conceive, the son, Joseph, was ill treated by his siblings because of the favor placed upon him by their father. He was eventually sold by his brothers into slavery in the land of Egypt according to Genesis. Later, it is Joseph, favored by the Pharaoh of Egypt and given a prominent position within his court, who comes to the rescue of his father's entire clan from a severe famine in the land of Canaan. The land from which Israel and his clan left to dwell in Egypt was called Haran of Togarmah. The narrative continues by explaining that Joseph married the daughter of an Egyptian priest and bore two sons, Manasseh and Ephraim. Ephraim apparently had four sons, but the second and third died or were killed early. It was a descendant of the fourth son, Joshua, who would play a major role in the Israelites' conquest of the land supposedly set aside for them by God, Canaan, and it is the line of Ephraim, through Joshua, from which the royal house of Israel is based.

This particular story, again the origin story of the Israelites, is found recounted in no other religious or ethnic tradition of any other group of people in any form or likeness or accepted as part of the canon of any other groups, except for Christians and Muslims, both faiths having sprung from the descendants of Abraham. Nevertheless, a remarkably parallel tale exists in the mythological origin stories of the Japanese. According to the Japanese origin tome, Ninigi, who was not supposed to inherit the earth because he was the second born son, did so, displacing his brother while his brother was preparing himself to come to earth. Therefore, it became Ninigi, and not his older brother, who was associated as the father of Japan and the Japanese people. The name that came to be used for the descendants of Ninigi is Yamato, a term for which several connections will be made later in the text. The place Ninigi resided is referred to as Takama-no-Hara (think Haran of Togarmah). The Japanese tale further describes how Ninigi fell in love with a woman named Konohana-sakuya-hime and tried to marry her before his father intervened, insisting that he marry the elder sister as well.

Like with Jacob and Rachel, Ninigi and Konohana-sakuya-hime were unable to have children together for a number of years. When Konohana-sakuya-hime finally does conceive – a son named Yamasachi-hiko – he is bullied by his older brothers, and eventually is cast out to the country of the sea god. Later, Yamasachi-hiko gains mystic powers which allow him to send a famine to the lands of his brothers (Yamato-no-kuni), but he would later repent of his transgression by helping his brothers.

Yamasachi-hiko goes on to marry a daughter of the priest of the sea god, and has a son, Ugaya-fukiaezu. Ugaya-fukiaezu has four sons, the second and third of which left at some point to other lands. The descendant of the fourth son is Emperor Jinmu, the conqueror of the land of Yamato, and the first of the line of the Japanese royal house. According to the specific story of Emperor Jinmu, a mythological creature called Yatagarasu, a magical or fiery eight-legged raven similar in imagery to the Phoenix and a deity of guidance, was sent from heaven to direct Jinmu and his people from the land of Kumano to Yamato. There are striking similarities between the tale of Yatagarasu helping Emperor Jinmu and the way by which the Israelites were guided from Egypt to Canaan. Could the Japanese tradition of Yatagarasu be a distorted version of the Biblical account of the Exodus, and the Lord of the Israelites sending quail at one point to help feed them along with a pillar in the sky to guide them?

Even the creation myth from the opening books of Genesis is paralleled in the creation story of the Japanese. According to the *Nihon Shoki*:

> Before the heavens and the earth came into existence, all was a chaos, unimaginable limitless and without definite shape or form... Aeon followed aeon, then lo, out of this boundless, shapeless mass something light and transparent rose up and formed heaven.

The phrasing of this passage is nearly identical to those lines of the opening scene in Genesis.

The goddess Amaterasu, instead of giving her oldest

son the earth for his inheritance, bestowed it upon her second son. While Genesis does not make clear the relationship between the Lord God and Lucifer in terms of which was the older of the two, the creation myth of the Sumerians and Babylonians is consistent with those of the Japanese and Jews in that the older brother was jealous of the younger, and that this was the basis of the feud between them in both heaven and earth. Some may argue that since the Japanese believe that Amaterasu is a deity personified as a female, this somehow debunks any connection these two mythologies may have. However, a couple of ancient sources actually identify Amaterasu as being male, rather than female.

The continuation of the stories found in the *Old Testament*, especially from the period of Saul, parallels that of the Japanese mythologies found in both the *Nihon Shoki* and *Kojiki*, for example.

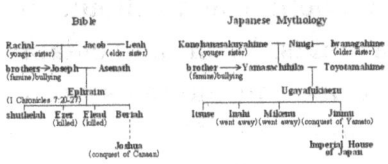

Fig. 2

The Exoduses

One of the most iconic epochs of the *Old Testament* is the migration story of the Israelites from Egypt, beginning with the tale of Moses reluctantly accepting the calling to be a prophet to the people, and his role in the departure, and subsequent wanderings of the people in the wilderness. This story is such a popular part of the Western Christian culture that Hollywood tried to mo-

43

netize the epoch, not once, but twice, with A-list celebrities playing the roles of the leading figures.

And the parallels between the *Nihon Shoki* and *Kojiki* with the *Torah* continue, with only small differences. Nearly all of the details in the tale according to the *Old Testament* and Japanese mythological sources, such as the place names (though, and expectedly, spelled differently due to differing contemporary languages), acts and deeds are the same. One of the major departures, however, is in the pronunciation and spelling of the names of the characters. There does not seem to be any similarity in the names of the supposedly corresponding characters. Some might choose to argue that this is one reason to dispel any correlation or connection between these two sets of mythologies. That is, however, short-sighted. Instead of expecting there to be some marginally recognizable similarity in the names in each set of traditions, one should expect the exact opposite. Any similarity in pronunciation or spelling at all should be considered remarkable, and a bonus. As already established, the deeds and actions described in the tales are the most important aspects of the stories. Dates and names are always the first details to get butchered in the cases of retelling stories over thousands of years. Even if the actions and deeds are modified or simplified, they still traditionally retain the basic framework of truth.

The biggest hurdle faced for some with reconciling the respective exodus stories in the *Torah* and ancient Japanese records, as it turns out, has nothing to do directly with the stories themselves, or whether or not they are arguably telling the same tales. The challenge comes from the long-term effect of hundreds of years of poor scholarship of the historical truths surrounding the Israelite Exodus, and more specifically with the belief and understanding of the path the Israelites may have taken in their journey from Egypt and eventual arrival to their promised land. Virtually every Biblical scholar or theologian, for as far back as there are recorded treatises on the subject, have believed, and still do believe, that the Israelites, after fleeing from captivity under the guidance of Moses, traveled due east, first across the desert, then across the Red Sea into the Sinai Peninsula, where they wandered for forty years before eventually finding their way into their promised land of Canaan.

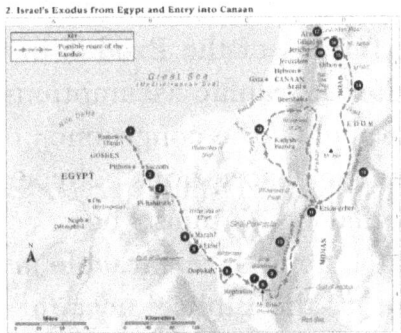

Fig. 3

Unfortunately, and as is made clear by Joseph Eidelberg in *The Japanese and the Ten Lost Tribes of Israel*, this conclusion is absolutely wrong and with no basis.

For hundreds of years, theologians and Biblical scholars have tried to map out the supposed route of the Israelites from their departure from Egypt, connecting the descriptions of that journey in the *Old Testament* with their corresponding contemporary locations. At nearly every turn these very same scholars could not, and have not, adequately reconciled the place names provided in the Exodus story with corresponding places between Egypt and the Sinai, with just a few exceptions. Yet, they consistently insist that despite the numerous incongruities it is not their scholarship that is lacking, but, instead, there must be some other as of yet unexplainable reason for the inaccuracies, rather than being open-minded to other possibility theories. Unfortunately, the arrogance of those who have and do study this topic has blinded them from the truth.

That truth is, and again the work of Joseph Eidelberg must be given full credit on this matter, that the Israelites did not move east from Egypt immediately, but in fact first migrated west across North Africa. When one takes the descriptions of the Exodus in the *Torah* and applies different geographic assumptions, as Eidelberg outlines so thoroughly, the congruency of place names and their respective descriptions between the *Bible* and Japanese texts that had hitherto been so elusive begin to suddenly match up with remarkable precision. It also becomes clear that the Biblical account of the Exodus details are not nearly as accurately preserved as scholars would hope them to be. Even more controversially, it becomes equally clear that early transcribers of the *Old Testament* completely changed some place names in order to fit the locations of places between the Nile River and Sinai with places they were either familiar with or thought corresponded to the place names identified in the story. For anyone interested in a full explanation of all of the myriad pieces of this puzzle that are finally put into place by Joseph Eidelberg, please read his book *The Japanese and the Ten Lost Tribes of Israel.*

The Lands of Inheritance

Eventually, the Israelites do begin to approach the lands they believe were ordained to be their inheritance. Emperor Jinmu, or perhaps Moses, according to the *Nihon Shoki* and *Kojiki*, gathered the elders together to show them a distant land to the east that was beautiful, full of resources, and which the gods had set aside for the people. He referred to this land as the Land of Reed Meadows on the other side of the Reed Sea and proposed that they settle in that land. Could the Reed Sea be the Red Sea, which was once correctly known as the Reed Sea?

After pondering his proposal, the princes agree to the plan. Ships were built to transport the people across a body of water, and then began slowly making their way as a group, stopping periodically along the way, until they eventually encountered the inhabitants of the Land of Reed Meadows. One of the first people they encountered put up significant resistance, and Emperor Jinmu and his people were repelled, forcing them to consider an alternative path to their destination. In their effort to find an alternative path, they got lost and wandered for many years in strange lands. When Amaterasu saw that her offspring were having trouble, She (or perhaps He) announced to Emperor Jinmu that She would send a divine crow (Eight-Legged Crow) to guide the people. With the help of this divine crow from heaven, the people were successful in eventually making their way out of the wilderness.

Once out of the wilderness, and back into the Land of Reed Meadow, the armies of Emperor Jinmu once again encountered fierce opposition to his people settling the land. One such group with which they did battle were the Yebisu warriors (Jebusites?). In their efforts to overtake the tribes of the Land of Reed Meadow, Emperor Jinmu's forces were aided by supernatural forces such as hailstorms and lightning storms. Thirty-seven years after the passing of Emperor Jinmu, his most trusted general, Ai-no-Ummi (Joshua), saw to the end of the conquest of the land of his people's birthright, Yamato.

A long period of time passed after Emperor Jinmu's death with very little details recorded. The tales eventually continue with that of Emperor Sujin (King David?). In the early years of Emperor Sujin's reign, the land suffered from several years of drought and famine. In an effort to seek guidance in how to deal with the calamity, Emperor Sujin invokes the spirit of the gods. Supposedly in a dream, Emperor Sujin is visited by the god of Yamato, and instructed to ordain a priest to the god of Yamato, which he did, appointing a man from Idomi (Edom?). It is said that about ten years later, a group from Idomi rose up (Adonijah?) against Emperor Sujin, for which he had to raise an army in order to first crush the opposition, and then restore order to the kingdom. Could this be the very same story of the Adonijah uprising that threatened King David from being able to appoint his son Solomon to the throne? Emperor Sujin apparently spent the remainder of his years dedicated to improving the quality of life and condition of his empire.

Just prior to his death, Emperor Sujin officially appointed his son Suinin (King Solomon?) as his successor. The choice of Suinin was based on his superior wisdom. The story is told that Suinin had a dream in which the solution to a tremendous shortage of grain was revealed to him. Emperor Suinin proved to be a pious emperor and built the first great shrine (Temple of Solomon?) along with expansive infrastructure projects that included vast

48

irrigation systems. The timeline described in the *Nihon Shoki* and *Kojiki* states that the descendants of Emperor Suinin were plagued by invasions and uprisings from neighboring tribes, and other internal and external conflicts, which weakened the empire over time. Eighty-three years after the death of the grandson of Emperor Suinin, the son of Prince Yamato-Dake, Chiuai, took the throne. Chiuai was apparently extremely handsome and large in stature. It is stated in the mythologies that he led his armies against a foe called Kumaso (Moab, or Kemosh in Hebrew?). Unfortunately, Emperor Chiuai (King Saul, first king of Israel?) died prematurely as a result of disobeying the word of the god of the Yamato.

Even someone with a marginal knowledge of the timeline of events and tales of the *Old Testament* will recognize that if Emperor Chiuai is the equivalent of King Saul, then there is a major discrepancy in the timeline found in the *Old Testament* versus the Japanese records. In fact, the *Nihon Shoki* and *Kojiki* seem to have confused a great many details, blending the Exile from Canaan with that across Asia to Japan. This becomes, therefore, a point of contention for many, and a reason to refute any and all relationship between the ancient tales between these two peoples. However (and a truth that cannot be ignored), any record of any kind of the antiquity of these documents will expectedly have inaccuracies scattered throughout their stories. Again, instead of being surprised that not all of the details line up perfectly, it should be expected that some will not. The *Nihon Shoki* and *Kojiki* are replete with confusions between very ancient histories and the details of events that came much later. This would be expected for an entire history that was lost in a tragic fire and which, when reproduced hundreds of

years later, could only rely on vague memories to trans-
cribe those histories. So, the Japanese records can, and
should, be forgiven for not being as precise as perhaps
the *Torah* is for its vintage. Dates are not important. Focus on the deeds and actions. For a much more detailed
and comprehensive study of these and many other details, it is recommended that the reader look further at
Prof. Shachan's work.

Uji or Lineage Groups

The tribal dynamics of the ancient Israelites, as far
back as the time of Jacob, were fairly peculiar, and remained unique even after some groups of Jews returned
from exile to the Holy Land. Despite the strong familial
ties which bound the early Israelites as a whole extended
family group – one people under covenant with their
Lord – the twelve distinct tribes which eventually developed out of the lineages that came from the seed of Jacob were from early on, and up to at least the First Exile,
fiercely independent. This feeling of independence was
so intense at times that animosity between some of the
tribes resulted in armed conflict. Interestingly, however,
when faced with exterior threats, these disparate tribes
somehow seemed to find it natural to bind together
in mutual support and protection more often than not.
Likewise, much of the shared cultural heritage provided
for as much of a sense of oneness as there were differences.

Internal relations, politics, and dynamics could be
quite prickly, but the face shown to the outside world
was one of relative unity and cohesion. This strange form
of cooperation or quasi-confederation, as awkward as it
was, worked, relatively speaking. Though, this wobbly

balance of function and dysfunction also explains why Israel remained a modest, marginal group on the fringes of Western Asia for hundreds of years with very little progress compared to their neighbors, and why the experiment with unification under a monarchy proved ultimately to fail after only a brief taste of development and empire. The unique tribal make-up of the early Jewish people was, nevertheless, a distinctive part of the overall characteristics of the people as a whole and was carried forward with them into exile and beyond.

On the other side of the globe, a nearly identical set of ancient tribal norms and historical phenomena would have been found on the islands of Japan, beginning with the transition from the Joumon period to the Yayoi. The migrants to the Japanese islands at the time, the Ainu among perhaps others, brought with them a very distinctive set of social, economic, political, and religious classifications as tribal entities. These groups, related by lineage, are referred to as *uji*. While each *uji* loosely shared some characteristics inherent in their common ancestry, they chose to remain independent from each other, only interacting, it seems, out of strict necessity. Like each of the Twelve Tribes of Israel prior to the imperial era, each *uji* would have been governed by a patriarch-chieftain. The land of a *uji* was understood to be the collective property of the clan, each family having the blessing to live and work on a portion.

The social, political, economic, and religious climate changed drastically with the arrival of the wave of Asiatic migrants, corresponding to the transition from the Yayoi to Yamato periods around the fourth century CE. These people – and argued by this author – a second wave of descendants of the Lost Tribes of Israel, already had a relatively established linguistic (Japanese), religious (Buddhism), political (Confucianism), and economic (feudalism) cohesiveness, identity, and stratification. These realities were promptly imposed upon the entirety of the islands over the several hundred years it took to subdue the indigenous *uji*. Therefore, feudalism and monarchy eventually replaced the *uji* confederacy and tribal chieftains.

This same development took place earlier in early Israel during the adoption of a monarchy. Despite most willingly submitting to a king, whose seat was eventually established in Jerusalem, many common Israelites resented the loss of their tribal independence, especially since that royal lineage was connected with the house of Judah. Like the Hata clan of the Yamato, the tribe of Judah will forever be associated with the monarchy of ancient Israel, for good or for bad. Did the descendants of the Lost Tribes of Israel from Samaria, resentful to the end of being chained to the yoke of a monarch, bring their insistence on independence and self-determination with them to the islands of Japan? Did a second wave of Israelites, led by the royalist house of Judah, follow several hundred years later, only to subdue their brothers and sisters once again?

Chapter 5
Shared Beliefs and Legal Traditions

The Taika Renewal and Ancient Jewish Laws (Book of the Covenant)

The first set of guiding principles and laws for the ancient Israelites is referred to as the Law of Moses, both in the initial decree as well as in what was added over time. The earliest set of universal laws governing the early Japanese was referred to as The Laws of Men and Women or the Renewal of Taika. In reviewing these two codes of law, one finds a large number of similar edicts and shared principles.

In early Japan, there came a time when there was a very real battle, both spiritual and political, for the hearts and minds of Japanese people and the nation as a whole around the fourth and fifth centuries CE. Those that supported the dominance of Buddhism, which had been gaining prominence on the islands from about the third or fourth century CE, led by the Soga clan, and those that remained loyal to Shintoism, led by the Mononobe clan, brought the country to civil war. This turmoil lasted for nearly two hundred years. For a time, the Buddhists reigned, but eventually the Shintoists prevailed, and oversaw an overall revival of Shintoism across the country from about 645 CE, if the records are accurate. This event is referred to as the Renewal of Taika and marked the beginning of the Taika era. This civil war which raged between the proponents of Shintoism and Buddhism respectively was not just a fight for the soul of Japan, but for its future political identity. In many ways Shintoism represented the domain of the rural peasant, the commoner, the farmer – an identity separate from the influence of the mainland of Asia – whereas Buddhism was associated with the growing urban elite and gentry with very close ties to the Chinese imperial regime. Likewise, the cultic struggle between support for Yahweh and Baal was very much rural versus urban; ruled vs those that ruled.

It should be noted that *taika* meant "hope" in early Japanese, as does *tikva* in Hebrew-Aramaic. What is interesting about the beginning of the Taika period is what is said of the first days of that era in the *Nihon Shoki*. According to the story, the new era was marked as beginning in the seventh month of the year, on the first day of the seventh month. This also happens to be the Jewish sacred day of the Holy Convocation. On the fourteenth day of this month messengers were sent out to every corner of the nation to make offerings to *kami*. Again, this coincides with the Jewish Feast of the Tabernacles. The fifteenth day marked a day of more feasting and celebration. This seems to coincide with the Jewish Passover preparations on the fourteenth and Passover celebrations on the fifteenth day of the seventh month of Nisan.

As part of the re-establishment of Shintoism to prominence, a number of religiously motivated initiatives were instituted. A law was passed early on in the period by which a census would be conducted, and the lands of the nation were to be redistributed to all people, which apparently continued in practice periodically until the 900s CE. First, the land was nationalized, and the redistribution of land was to take place after every six years, or during every seventh year. The land was to be divided out according to the size of each household. Was this the same practice as in ancient Egypt whereby the land farmed for six years was left to rest for the seventh, and land inheritance during the imperial period of Israel was determined according to the size of the population of each family group?

For nearly all scholars on this matter, the Taika policies are said to have been a byproduct of the Confucian influence coming out of China at the time. However, anyone even vaguely familiar with Confucian principles must admit that there is nothing even remotely Confucian in nature about the Taika-era laws. When evaluated without a bias toward Confucianism, though, one discovers many legal parallels between the customs of ancient Israel and those established during the Taika era.

Taika Era Policy (Nihon Shoki)	Jewish Legal Custom (Torah)
If slaves of two houses marry, the children of this marriage shall belong to the mother (p. 202).	Exodus 21:4
Collect double from the one who got unjustly.	Exodus 22:9

People shall not cut their hair and stab themselves when mourning over their deal relatives (p. 220).	Leviticus 21:5
Husbands should not accuse their wives of adultery if they cannot prove their case with…let us say, three credible witnesses (p. 221).	Deuteronomy 17:6
If a man left his horse in charge of a farmer, and the farmer falsely claimed that the horse had died, or had been stolen – he could often clear himself of all responsibility by doing purgation; the "reform" suggests that a village elder be a witness when handing the horse for stabling (pp. 222-23).	Exodus 22:10-11
When a wife commits adultery he must divorce her.	Deuteronomy 24:1
There are many cases of persons who, having seen, say that they have not seen, or who, having not seen, say that they have seen, or who, having heard say that they have not heard, or who, having not heard say that they have heard, being deliberate liars, and devoid of truth in words and in sight (p. 220).	Leviticus 19:11

For each ward in the capital let there be appointed one alderman, and for four wards one chief alderman, who shall be charged with the superintendence of the population and the examination of criminal matters (p. 207).	Deuteronomy 16:18
The sale of land shall not be allowed (p. 205)	Leviticus 25:23
Again, there are cases when people have applied to others for the loan of pots to boil rice, and the pots have knocked against something and have been upset. Upon this the owner of the pot compels purgation to be made (p. 222).	Exodus 22:14
Those who convert property to their own use shall be mulcted in double its value (p. 213).	Exodus 22:14

Atonement

The act of atoning – or casting away – of one's sins is one of several atypical Jewish principles at the heart of the faith. The general belief holds that every person sins from time to time and must account for those sins before one passes away so as to be worthy to enter the presence of God for eternity. From early in the Jewish tradition there were two formal times during which the body of faithful collectively participated in ceremonies that supposedly cleansed the faithful of their sins. These ritual days were on the first day of the seventh month and the first day of the first month; the Feast of the Booths and Passover respectively (Leviticus 16).

One aspect of these celebrations was the ritual of the scapegoat performed by the high priest of the Temple at Jerusalem. The high priest would give a prayer while laying his hands on the head of a goat by which the priest symbolically transferred the sins of the people into the goat. The goat would be subsequently taken into an uninhabited wilderness and released, and thus, metaphorically, God would not see the people's sins anymore. The more modern use of the term "scapegoat" and its meaning has its origins in this ancient Jewish practice.

There were similar rituals and practices in ancient Shintoism. The idea of periodically "atoning" for one's sins was very much a key component to the early canon of Shintoism and took form in the *ooharai*. The *ooharai* were ceremonies of ritualistic cleansing, some of which will be touched on later in the book in detail. It was believed that these ceremonies helped wash away both the sins of the people and nation. The emperor (think priestly king) would officiate these bi-annual ceremonies. As already established, the Shinto customs of the days of celebration are remarkably similar to the Feast of Booths and Jewish Passover. As in Judaism, which also follows the Lunar Calendar for religious purposes, the Shinto religious calendar would also have originally been based on the cycles of the moon, and, therefore, these holy events would have varied in terms of when they fell throughout any given year. Now, however, and since the Lunar Calendar is no longer generally used in Japan, they take place yearly on July 1 and January 1, respectively.

During these ceremonies at shrines of the imperial family, the emperor would wear a set of new white-linen garments – a symbol of humility and purity – and recite a prayer in which he asked for blessings for the people and nation, and for the cleansing of the sins of the people and nation. It was believed that during the ritual the emperor's linen garments would symbolically absorb all of the sins, and after the ceremony, these garments would be thrown into a river for the sins to float away out of sight. The Japanese people in attendance of these rituals would be given a piece of white paper for them to cut, or otherwise form, into the shape of a man and throw into a river, also metaphorically casting their supposed sins away. This practice is known as *nagashibina*, and in some cases the people will cast dolls that are believed to possess one's sins into a river instead of a shaped piece of paper. While the strictly physical form of the *nagashibina* in Shintoism and scapegoat in Judaism are not the same, the symbolism and intentions are exactly the same.

Additionally, the types of taboos mentioned in the prayer in the Shinto tradition and that mentioned to have been part of the Jewish ceremony as outlined in Leviticus are essentially the same: harming another person, defiling a dead body, leprosy, being hunchback, sexual intercourse with one's mother or other forms of incest, rape, bestiality, magic or sorcery, etc.

Taboos Versus Sins

The concept of "sin" or "sinfulness" is well understood in Judaism, as it is in Christianity and Islam, and even within evolved forms of Buddhism, and this doctrine plays a central role in those traditions. The general idea within these religions is that the violation of God's or the gods' principles, laws, teachings, etc. constitute a violation of the commitment, promise, relationship, and/ or spiritual contract one has with God or the gods. This sin, and the person that committed it, therefore, must receive a consequence, either spiritual or physical in nature. And, if one did not "atone" for their sins, then that individual may not be able to exist after death in the presence of God or some form of afterlife. Due in part to the widespread and dominant role that Christianity and Islam have played globally, especially from the beginnings of the various Islamic kingdoms in Asia and of European exploration and colonization in the fifteenth century CE, the belief that a person can and does sin has become almost universal.

Thus, many people incorrectly assume that Judaism, from which Christianity derives many of its precepts, has precisely the same traditional understanding of "sin." While this may arguably be the case today in Judaism's more current iteration, it was not so in its earliest form.

Man's fall became a basic to holy teaching only through certain speculations of early Christendom. They were based upon conceptions which were undeniably derived from Oriental gnosis, but were alien to genuine Israelite piety.

It was true that Yahweh, God, forbade the faithful from doing certain things, or commanded that they do others. The major difference was that doing something that was forbidden or prohibited, or not doing something that was required, was not considered a sin in the sense that it blemished a person's soul, but, rather, a personal vice, and something for which a person should atone through making offerings at the Temple, or another shrine, for example. Ritual purification was also another way by which someone could reconstitute their relationship with God.

This was one of the purposes of visiting a *mikveh*, for example, to receive periodic purification from the cleansing properties of the water. Interestingly, the practice of baptism by water, which is a very Christian sacrament, has its roots in the Jewish ritual of purification in a sacred body of water. There was no implied divine moral judgment associated as in the Christian or Islamic idea of "sin." Unlike in Christianity or Islam in which judgment is imposed continually in this earthly existence, and that verdict has supposedly eternal consequences in addition to mortal ones, it was generally understood by both early Jews and Shintoists that violating prescribed norms would incur the punishment of the gods in various tangible and experienced ways such as famine, disease, and/or natural disasters.

Murder, lying, stealing, and the like, while they are supposedly first proclaimed to Moses as "inadvisable", and which were later codified on the stone tablets known as the Ten Commandments, were understood to incur the wrath of God and considered violations of the social contract one has with the community. These were not punished by any organization or religious body, but were, however, addressed by the civil authorities. Thus, murder, for example, was a capital offense as far as the law of the land was concerned. Doctrinally, in early Judaism, so long as a person made restitution or recommitted themselves to God, along with the proper sacrifices, that person could in theory regain the favor of God. Judaism does not acquire its puritanical notions of "mortal sin" as carried forward by Christianity and Islam until the post-Exilic period. This drive toward a more conservative interpretation, while periodically present before the Exile, may, like Shintoism's response to Buddhism in the centuries leading up to the Taika era, have been a coarse correction overcompensating for the threats faced to survival and relevance of the faith.

The Jewish understanding of things that the Lord had deemed forbidden (*chattah*) is very much in line with the Shinto concept of taboos, or *tsumi*. As described later in the book, there were several examples of taboos, such as menstruating women visiting shrines or participating in any rituals of any kind, or of having contact with the body of a deceased person. Again, there was no moral connotation connected to these. Therefore, if someone did have contact with a corpse, for example, they could simply undergo a ritualistic cleansing in order to rid themselves of any impurities that contact may have passed on to a person's *ki*, or life force. As in Judaism, a person was never considered morally lacking for their actions as is often the case in Christianity and Islam. And, therefore, it was not the community of believers or priesthood that would judge whether someone would or would not reside in heaven after death but the authority of God alone.

The clear lack of or a defined sense of "sin" in Shintoism and Judaism may be rooted in the fact that both faiths did not have a clear tradition of differentiating "good" versus "evil." Again, many wrongly conclude that Judaism is the doctrinal source of the Christian and later Islamic ideas of the eternal struggle of good versus evil. This is not the case. The more contemporary form of Judaism, along with Christianity and Islam, gets its understanding on this topic, in part, based on influences coming out of more eastern spiritual systems, as is the case with Babylon on Judaism during the Exile.

Feelings Toward Male-Female Relations

One might assume that early Judaism was rather conservative and strict when it came to sexual relations between men and women, based on the Christian and Islamic derivatives thereof, or of the more contemporary form of Judaism that first came out of the Exile. This was not the case, or at least not consistently so, from the earliest iterations of the faith under Abraham, or any period up until the Exile. The conservative nature of our modern world as it relates to relations between men and women was – and still is – rooted in the later interpretation of Jewish law and doctrine and the rise and dominance of Christian and Islamic principles globally; one of several byproducts or legacies of colonialism.

The truth is that Semitic peoples of Western Asia had very different ideas of decorum when it came to what was acceptable between men and women. It was acceptable for a man, according to his financial means, to have more than one wife. This was not culturally the exclusive right of royalty or of some aristocracy, but of all men. Abraham, for example, and there are dozens of cases described in the *Bible* like it, had several wives at any one time. This was not considered sinful. Rather, having more than one wife was seen as a show of status. Even what constituted the act of getting married differs drastically from what the modern world understands that to mean. The *Old Testament* tells us that when a man wanted to wed a woman he would simply "take her" as his wife. This does not always mean that a man proposed marriage. While a woman in some rare cases may have agreed to her union with her husband, in most cases a man made a financial arrangement with a woman's father or male guardian, or he literally just took her, as in he forced himself upon a woman he wanted.

A man having sexual intercourse with a woman before a formal union was agreed upon, however it came about, while unfavorable and perhaps incurring the anger of a woman's family, was not considered a sin, and, therefore, was not believed to incur any kind of spiritual response from a deity, whether it be Yahweh, Baal, or other. Rather, culturally speaking, this was considered a commitment of a man to take a woman as his wife, and to be a reliable provider for her and any children from the union. If a man did have relations with a woman, and then did not fulfill the responsibilities of a husband, he could be punished by the family of the wife. Again, there was not a formal consequence prescribed based on any religious doctrine or codified principles.

Adultery, committed by men, while certainly not encouraged and definitely frowned upon, was not treated as sinful or punished. If any blame or punishment were to actually be given it was often the woman that was held responsible. Take the case of King David and Bathsheba. If we are to believe the Biblical story, King David wanted to take a woman named Bathsheba as his wife based on seeing her bathing. The only issue was that Bathsheba was already married to an officer serving in King David's army. In order to be able to wed Bathsheba, he had her husband, and his officer, Uriah, moved to the front lines of a battle, which resulted in him being killed in combat. According to the story, King David was not punished by God for coveting another man's wife, but for placing the husband in harm's way unnecessarily so that he would be killed, and, thus, release Bathsheba to become one of his already large number of wives.

This very informal nature of what constitutes a man and a woman entering into the union of marriage, for example, is quite unique, even in the ancient world, especially if one compares it to neighboring religious traditions in Egypt, Sumer/Babylon/Assyria, and further east in India and China. The practices of early peoples of Japan and ancient Shintoism were very similar, especially when one looks at the Ainu customs and spirituality (see Chapter 11). It was not until Buddhism took a much stronger hold of the culture, and began blending with Shintoism, that the traditions began changing. It is true that Shintoism has a very formal marriage ceremony, but that only came about as a heavily syncretized ritual influenced by and in competition with Buddhism. Even the partially Buddhist ceremony of early Japan, or *kekkonshiki*, would be unrecognizable to Japanese today, due in part to the heavy syncretic influence of later waves of Christian influences on such rituals.

Chapter 6
Traditions of the Priesthood

In the Shinto tradition, the term for the priests is
shinshoku, or servant of the gods, and was in ancient
times a calling passed down from father to son. In the
Jewish faith, the priests are referred to as *cohen*, and collectively as *cohenim*, and were connected to a variety of
sib, or cohorts of priests, for numerous cultic traditions.
The Jewish priesthood was also hereditary. The language
of the *Old Testament* gives the impression that there was
a very coherent and uniform nature to the priestly class of
ancient Judaism, under the direction of the house of Levi,
and the descendants of Moses' brother Aaron. This was
not the case. Rather, there was a combination of priesthoods, or *sib*, each devoted to one of many Western Asian
deities, or, as referred to collectively in the *Torah*, Baal;
one of which was the Yahweh cult. While each of these
various cultic groups had some distinctive features and
individual characteristics, they also shared a great many
things which gave them a collectively similar look and feel.
This would have been very much the case with the ancient
Shinto priesthoods as well; sharing a cumulative spiritual

heritage while still maintaining their own peculiarities.

Priestly Robes

With the exception of the high priest, who wore robes of color – such as sky blue – the ordinary priests of Levi, and the kings of Israel officiating in a ritual, wore robes of simple white linen. This is precisely the same tradition of the Shinto priests of Japan, or *shinshoku*, and Japanese emperors when participating in Shinto rituals, for which white is considered the holiest color, representing purity. Some *shinshoku* to this day wear robes of blue and white when performing ceremonies, like their Jewish counterparts. Rabbi Marvin Tokayer, who lived for ten years in Japan, and studied Shintoism extensively, confirmed that the robes of the Shinto priests resemble what is described of the Israelite priests in the *Old Testament*.

Both the priestly robes of Shintoism and Judaism have tassels or pieces of fringe about ten inches long hanging from the corners of the robes (Deuteronomy 22:12). A linen *ephod*, a rectangular cloth worn over the robe, hanging from the shoulders to thighs, was worn by the ordinary priests of Israel, as it is, and was, by Shinto priests. Additionally, both sets of priests wore a cap on their heads, along with a sash tied around their waists.

Fig. 4 - picture of Shinto priests

Fig. 5 - drawing of a Levite high priest

Priestly Instruments

Seven weeks before the celebration of Shavuot (Pentecost) and at Sukkot (Feast of Booths), Jewish priests would gather a bundle or sheaf of the first fruits of the grain harvest. Once gathered, these sheaves would then be used to wave before the people in order to symbolically sanctify a person, place, or thing. This same act was undertaken by the priests of Shintoism in ancient times, gathering grain shoots of the first harvest into a bundle for purification rituals. Now, Shinto priests use a modified form of the sheaf of grain in the form of what is called an *ounusa*, also referred to as *oharagushi* – a collection of paper made to look like a bundle of grain.

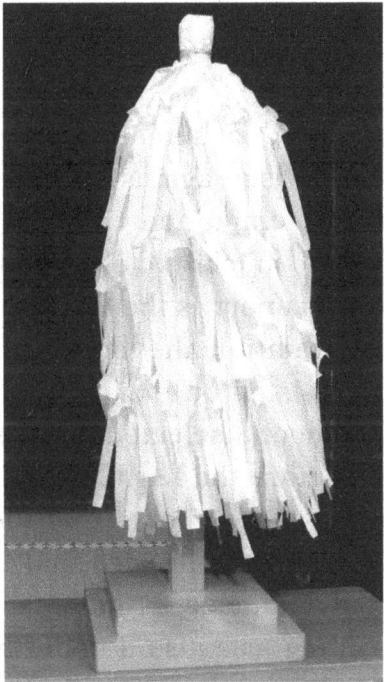

Fig. 6 - picture of an ounusa

Fig. 7 - drawing of a Levite priest holding a harvest sheaf

Priestly Kingship

The Israelites were, on numerous occasions and by various prophets, advised against raising a king before them. However, the temptation to appoint a king over them proved to be too much, and eventually a man by the name of Saul was set apart as the first king of Israel. According to Jewish tradition, the Israelites were admonished that if they insisted on having a king they should at least choose someone selected for the role by God; someone humble before the Lord. Thus began a history among the Israelites of the belief that their kings were essentially priestly kings. The idea that the monarch is somehow selected, endowed, or set apart by a deity or deities for the calling was also a belief held by the Japanese people from ancient times. Even before the political momentum shifted away from the position of the emperor as the supreme power of the land, and was, for a time, held in reality by generations of the Fujiwara clan, and later, various *shougun*, or supreme military com-

manders of the *bakufu* system (administrative govern-
ments led by military dictators from the time of Mina-
moto Yoritomo in the twelfth century), the emperor was
still believed to be the spiritual representative of heaven
on earth. As such, both the emperors of Japan and the
kings of Israel played a role in religious ceremonies (1
Chronicles 15:27). For this, they both would have, like the
priests of their respective traditions, worn vestments of
white linen.

Fig. 8

Priestly Rituals

Like the members of any priesthood of any religious
denomination, whether formal or informal, the *shinshoku*
of Shintoism perform various rituals (*saishi*) at the places
of worship, or shrines (*jinja, miya,* or *yashiro*). In the case
of Shintoism, there are eleven distinct rituals performed.
Typical rituals performed include:

> *jichinsai:* A ceremonial blessing of a new buil-
> ding or home with the purpose of purifying it.

norito: A prayer recited on behalf of the faithful to a *kami* (deity/spirit).

ooharai: Refers to a set of purification rites performed by anyone before entering a *jinja* or participating in a *matsuri*, or Shinto religious festival/ceremony. In both faiths there is a strong tradition requiring the priests, for example, to wash their clothes and bathe in freshwater before performing their duties. Salt is used in both Judaism and Shintoism for purifying shrines or other holy places. Salt has other similar uses such as welcoming guests with it, sanctifying a feast, or bathing a newborn child.

naorai: Sacrificial offerings made of food to the *kami*. In ancient times these may have been animal sacrifices, but are now in the form of fruits, grains, liquor, etc. (Exodus 25:29-30, Leviticus 23:13). The offerings made are, like in Judaism, supposed to be of the first fruits. After the offerings are made there is usually a feast (*naorai* feast). In ancient times the priests would consume the offerings (Numbers 18:11).

matsuri: Shinto priests officiate various important religious ceremonies in which entire communities are expected to participate; *kanname-sai* (festival of first fruits), *juugyo-ya* (Feast of Booths), *natsu matsuri* (similar to the Jewish Passover).

shinzen kekkon: Priests officiate weddings that resemble the ancient marriage customs of the Israelites.

These rites and rituals are virtually the same as would have been witnessed thousands of years ago at either the early desert Tabernacle or at the later Temple of Solomon.

Yamabushi

In both Judaism and Shintoism there are traditions of hermitic, ultra-devout, hybridized sects that, while claiming a relationship with the mother faith, are in and of themselves relatively unique in practice. There is a relatively unheard-of syncretic faith unique to Japan called Haguro Shugendo, an amalgamation of Shinto, Zen Buddhism, Japanese Taoism, and other animistic characteristics. The hermit priests and practitioners of this spiritual tradition are referred to as *yamabushi*, and in ancient times these ascetics chose to live isolated in the mountains devoted entirely to prayer, meditation, and perfecting their devotion, practicing a form of asceticism. Judaism has a long history of its own forms of mystics referred to collectively as *nebiim*. *Nebiim* traditionally lived in small, isolated groups in the mountains, dedicated to the rituals and practices of extreme devotion that was meant to connect one on a higher plane of spirituality. Many *nebiim* mystics lived or live a semi-monastic or communal lifestyle, dedicated entirely to their lifelong pursuit of applying these ascetic mysteries to unlocking a greater connection with the realm of the gods. Like the Shinto *yamabushi*, the *nebiim* were not all devoted to a single deity, but were, rather, found to be associated with

73

a variety of gods.

While *nebiim* mystics do not have a distinctive set of garments, the *yamabushi* priests do. Their vestments are remarkably similar to that of both the Shinto and Jewish priesthood, with several remarkable extras. In addition to all of the characteristic outfits of the Jewish or Shinto priesthood, the *yamabushi* also adorns a small black box on his forehead that is tied at the back of the head, called a *tokin*. *Tokin* are in form and function that of the phylactery (*tefillin*) in Judaism. Shintoism and Judaism are the only faiths with a tradition of this object.

Fig. 9 - picture of a yamabushi priest

Fig. 10 - drawing of a Levite priest

Yamabushi also carry and use a hollowed-out seashell (*horagai*), which is blown for various reasons at ceremonies. This is not unlike the ram's horn of the Israelite priests called the *shofar*. It is entirely possible that the seashell was used in the place of a ram's horn as sheep were not found in Japan in ancient times.

Fig. 11 - picture of a yamabushi blowing into a horagai

Fig. 12 - picture depicting a Jewish priest blowing into a shofar

The role of topography seems to be important both for the priests of Shintoism, Haguro Shugendo, and Judaism, with "high places" being of particular importance. The holiest places for these faiths are usually found at the tops of mountains or hills. The *Old Testament* is filled with story after story of the prophets communing with or receiving instructions from God on a mountaintop, such as Moses and the burning bush. There is a story in Japanese mythology of a *tengu*, something like a spirit, who dwelled high up on a mountain top, and a *ninja* who climbed this high mountain in search of receiving special abilities. According to the story, the *tengu* gave the *ninja* a tora no maki, or scroll of the *tora*, after giving him the special powers he requested. This tale has a surprising number of characteristics of the story of Moses and the Ten Commandments. Like the *tengu* connection to "high places" and their reverence for them, the Israelites, too, placed special importance on mountains.

The symbol of the *tengu* is supposedly a design remarkably similar to that of the Star of David. While the mythology surrounding the *tengu* describes them as some kind of spirit being, early Japanese paintings depicting *tengu* show them as flesh and blood people that happen to have large noses, much like on the ritual masks associated with the ancient Hata clan. *Tengu* also have a strong association with the *yamabushi* hermit priests and are often depicted wearing the very same ornamental attire as the *yamabushi*, including the customary phylactery similar to Jewish priests. Could the collective mythology about *tengu* be nothing more than twenty-five hundred years' worth of misunderstanding, incorrectly told oral traditions, etc, but were in fact members of the priestly elite that migrated with the rest of the descendants of the Lost Tribes of Israel and held a place of reverence among that people? Could the remnants of the *yamabushi* priesthood and the traditions of the *tengu* be based on the same thing? Could the *tora* scroll handed down from a *tengu* to an initiate, as depicted in art in recorded stories, be the very same *Torah* scroll Israelite priests pass on to newly initiated priests?

Fig.13 – a tengu depicted in Japanese art

Chapter 7

Parallels Between Shinto Shrines and Jewish Tabernacle/Temple

---

V irtually all faiths across time have had some form of holy center or sanctuaries of worship, from various temple complexes to churches and cathedrals. While there are often a number of consistent themes shared between all such places as understood by their overall purpose, there are usually additional consistencies in the physical or visible characteristics. This is most obvious in the universality of pyramid structures found in cultures in nearly every corner of the earth in the ancient world. Despite seeming to be on the opposite end of the spiritual spectrum, there are some rather striking commonalities between the sacred spaces of Shintoism, *jinja*, and the early tabernacles, and later the first and second temples of Judaism.

Location

Both the *jinja* of Shintoism and the temples built by the Israelites in Jerusalem were built upon hills (Mt. Moriah at the heart of Jerusalem). Nearly every mountain in Japan has some form of a shrine, and in ancient Israel, many mountain tops had informal places of worship, or "high places," such as described by the many traditions in the *Old Testament* in which prophets ascend to the top of a mountain to converse with or receive guidance from God. In both traditions, it is believed that mountain tops are special because they are closer to God or the spirit realm.

Fig. 14 - picture of Temple Mount or Mount Moriya

Fig. 15 - picture of a Shinto shrine

As supposedly commanded by God, the Israelites, whenever they pitched the Tabernacle, and later when constructing the first and second temples of Solomon, arranged it so that the entrance gates were on the east to receive the rising sun first, with the inner sanctums on the western side. This is also the case with nearly all Shinto shrines.

Overall Layout, Structure, and Construction

The general layout of both sacred places of worship is the same, even down to the approximate dimensions of the courtyards and inner sanctums, and as stated earlier, the placement thereof. The structural parts of the tabernacle, and later the internal framework of Solomon's Temple, were built exclusively of cedar wood, just as was and still is the case with Shinto shrines. Due to the lack of cedar in abundance in the Holy Land, it was imported from Lebanon. Cedar is more than abundant in Japan. Another construction feature with an apparent similarity is in the absence of any mortar or cut stones. According to the commandment given to Moses in the building of holy places, cut stones and mortar were forbidden. While we do not have any evidence for a stipulation in Shintoism, no stones used in *jinja* are cut or mortar applied.

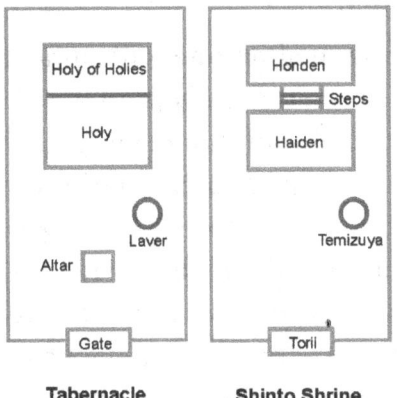

Tabernacle   **Shinto Shrine**

Fig. 16

A visitor to a Shinto shrine and, if it were possible, to the Jewish Tabernacle or Temple of Solomon will be greeted first by the entrance gate. In a Shinto *jinja*, the gate is called a *torii*. In both cases, the gates of the early tabernacle and the Shinto *jinja* take the form of two pillars with a crossbeam stretched across at the top between them.

After having passed through the gates and entering the courtyard, the first thing that one would encounter, in the case of the Jewish Tabernacle, would be the altar. The altar was used for making offerings in the form of animal sacrifice of the firstborn (i.e., sheep). This is a feature not found within a Shinto shrine complex. In fact, there is no tradition of animal sacrifice in Shintoism. If Shintoism is in fact a derivative of early Judaism, then this may not be as odd as it initially seems. According to the *Old Testament*, the Jews were commanded to not make animal sacrifices to the Lord except at the Tabernacle/Temple. Therefore, it is possible that the lack of an altar at Shinto shrines has more to do with the obedience of the early Jewish settlers to Japan rather than with a weak connection with Judaism.

Passing the brazen altar, one will come next to the *laver* in the Tabernacle, and *temizuya* in a Shinto shrine. The laver was essentially an elaborate washbasin at which Israelite priests stopped to conduct the ritualistic washing and purification before entering the inner sanctuary of the temple. *Temizuya* provide the exact same function within Shinto *jinja*. It is believed by both that the water in these respective basins has been sanctified and can, therefore, cleanse both the body and soul. The big exception, in this case, is that only the Levite priests would have practiced ablutions at the *laver*, while within the Shinto faith, all worshipers or visitors alike may cleanse themselves at the *temizuya*, at least that is the case in the modern iteration of Shintoism.

Fig. 17 – drawing of the temizuya at a Shinto shrine

Fig. 18 – drawing of the laver at the tabernacle/Temple of Solomon

In fact, only the Levite priests could enter the Tabernacle or later temple grounds, whereas the only restriction for visitors to the shrines of Shintoism is that of the innermost sanctum.

When a supplicant has finished purifying themselves, they will move westward toward the holiest portion of the property. Unless one is an initiate into the Shinto priesthood, one will be stopped by a short fence that separates the inner courtyard from the sacred shrine. This portion of the complex is referred to as the *heiden*. It is at this point that the common Shinto faithful stop for prayer facing the shrine's interior. The Temple of Solomon had a very similar barrier as well, past which lesser priests could not pass.

Fig. 19 – heiden

Crossing past the *heiden*, one would then move on toward the innermost structure of a Shinto *jinja*. Before stepping up to the gate of the entrance of this most sacred space, one is met by two statues of lions on the right and left. The statues of lions were found guarding Solomon's throne, just like these *komainu* still do for the Shinto *jinja*. The only differences between the use of these statues of these two faiths in their temples are that there were twelve (six on each side of the steps going into the inner sanctum, representing the twelve tribes of Israel) on guard at Solomon's throne, and only two at most Shinto shrines, and that these carvings were not found at the Temple of Solomon or the earlier Tabernacle. What makes this particular feature of the shrines and temples interesting is that lions are not native to Japan, and the native peoples of Japan would have had absolutely no knowledge of such animals. The image of the lion, and any iconographic importance that animal may have had, would have been introduced to the Japanese or brought to the islands from an outside source.

Fig. 20 – artist's depiction of the throne of David

Fig. 21 – picture of the komainu statues at the entrance to the Holy Place and Holy of Holies of a Shinto shrine

Another feature of the *jinja* complex is the administrative outbuilding called the *shamusho*. Every Shinto shrine has one from which the priests operate. Consequently, all Jewish synagogues have administrative offices called *shamashut*.

Holy Interior Sanctuaries

The innermost portion of both the Jewish Tabernacle/ Solomon's Temple and Shinto shrines is the holiest part, and, therefore, the most exclusive. In both faiths, only the priests with the highest level of initiation of the respective traditions are allowed into this most sanctimonious space. Upon approaching this part of these holy grounds, with the guardian lions keeping vigilant watch, a set of steps carry the priests up to the gateway. This building, according to the directions referenced in the *Old Testament*, was to be thirty feet long by fifteen feet wide. According to Dr. Jenichiro Oyabe, who was interviewed on this subject for the *Japan Advertiser* newspaper in 1929, these dimensions are supposedly the same as that of the earliest Shinto shrines. Kubo Arimasa also argues that the measurements of both were precisely the same. This cannot be confirmed, however, and is not evident among the collective *jinja* today.

These holy buildings are both divided into two parts, the Holy Place (*haiden*), or oratory, and the Holy of Holies (*honden*). The primary structural difference between Shintoism and Judaism is that the two parts of the Shinto form of the building are, in some cases, divided into two smaller buildings, while these two parts were separated merely by a cloth veil in both the Tabernacle and Temple of Solomon. The *haiden*, or Holy Place, of both respective traditions is the portion of this most sacred building in which the priests perform the daily ceremonies, prayers, and other rituals. The *honden*, or Holy of Holies, is believed to be the sacred hall in which God/spirits, or *kami*, reside. Only the high priest may enter the Holy of Holies, and only for the most important religious ceremonies, usually just once a year.

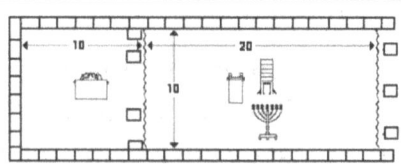

Fig. 22 – Diagram of the Holy Place and Holy of Holies from Solomon's Temple

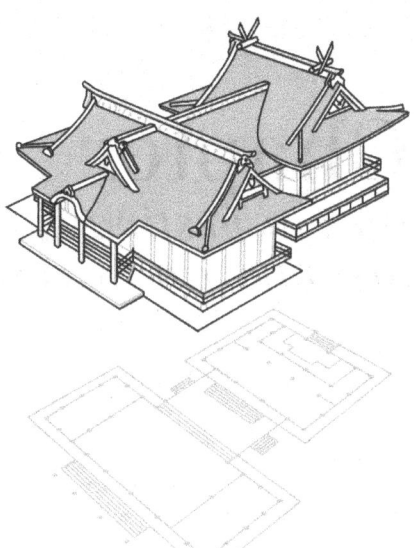

Fig. 23 – Diagram of the Holy Place and Holy of Holies of a Shinto shrine

Before a Shinto priest enters this most holy of sanctuaries, he/she will first ring a golden bell that is hung
from the entrance. This is very similar to the tradition
within Judaism in which Aaron, and the Levite priests
descended from his line, rang a "bell of gold" before entering the Holy Place so as not to die when doing so.

Chapter 8
Similarities in Festivals, Celebrations, Customs, and Ceremonies

M ost religious traditions, formally institutionalized or otherwise, are usually highly ritualized, with various forms of ceremonies, sa-
cred rites, and/or practices believed to bring the priestly
classes, and in some cases the congregants or believers,
to a closer connection or higher spiritual relationship
with a deity or deities. This is no less the case with both
Judaism and Shintoism. What makes these two faiths
unique, however, is the numerous ceremonial traditions
that share so many similarities. There is not merely one,
single, correlative rite, but numerous that resemble each
other, and, thus, should be explored to understand what,
if any, are the reasons for these common traits.

Omikoshi as the Arch of the Covenant

The single, most recognizable artifact, and lasting icon
of early Judaism, and perhaps even of the icons of this
very day, is the Ark of the Covenant, the device which
God supposedly instructed the Israelites to build in order to house the Ten Commandments (among other

items), and the vessel that the spirit of God is believed to have occasionally inhabited, and through which communicate. There are several reasons why this device or artifact was, and is, a central piece of the lore of Judaism:

> • According to the *Bible*, it was a commandment directly from God not just to build, but to do so to a very specific set of instructions.
> • This object was to house the tablets that supposedly had the Ten Commandments inscribed on them. Again, based on the text of the *Old Testament*, this was a direct communication to Moses from God.
> • There was a great deal of mystery and fear surrounding the Arch. It was believed, and described on several occasions in the *Bible*, to possess unspeakable power. So much so, that if properly handled, or touched, it would unleash death.
> • This was supposedly the vessel through which God would communicate to future generations of the priesthood, and the object which would hold the spirit of God on those occasions.

Fig. 24 – Modern replica of the Ark of the Covenant described in the Old Testament.

It is therefore obvious why this artifact would play a prominent role in both the passive and active aspects of the Jewish faith from the time of Jacob as the prophet until the time that it went missing. The Ark of the Covenant was a central feature of the early versions of the Tabernacle, and later the Temple of Solomon, in which it was placed prominently within the Holy of Holies, by which the priests could supposedly receive revelation from God. It played an important part in ceremonies whereby the Ark was carried through communities, door to door, and was believed to spiritually benefit the people in the process. It was also used almost like a spiritual talisman by the Israelite armies when going into battle, by which the Israelites believed that the power and presence of God would lead them to victory over their enemies. The irony of the latter is, of course, that according to the Biblical account, the Ark was ultimately lost after being captured by the Philistines after the Israelites went to war against them despite being directed by God through his prophet not to.

Fig. 25 – Artist's depiction of the Levite priests carrying the Ark of the Covenant.

If Judaism and Shintoism share common roots, then, based on the significant importance of the Ark in early Judaism, Shintoism must have a tradition of a similar object which played, and plays, a similar spiritual role.

And there is. It is referred to as an *omikoshi* in Japanese.

Fig. 26

Just as the Ark was an important physical part of the worship and spiritual lives of the early Israelites, *omikoshi* play an equally central role in the celebratory aspects of Shintoism. While *omikoshi* are not identical to what is described as the Ark of the Covenant, often differing in size and some stylistic features, the similarities of the overall form and function between these two objects cannot be denied.

Practitioners and the Shinto faithful believe *omikoshi* are sacred extensions of the shrines themselves, vessels by which *kami* are housed and carried when not residing within their respective Holy of Holies. *Omikoshi* are, therefore, housed in the Holy of Holies of their corresponding shrines when not used ceremonially outside of the shrines. As with Judaism, only the senior priests within the faith can enter the Holy of Holies to pray and worship, and thus be in the presence of *omikoshi*. However, several times a year during Shinto ceremonies, *omi-*

koshi play a featured role in the festivities. Men from the communities in and around Shinto shrines participating in the reverie will meet at the shrines and carry *omikoshi* on their shoulders out into their communities. While the Ark would have been carried exclusively by Levite priests, all male members of the community may help with this task. On several such occasions your author was lucky enough to have been included.

Fig. 27

There was one and only one Ark of the Covenant, whereas in Shintoism each *kami* can in theory have its own *omikoshi* or several. As part of the overall ceremonies, *omikoshi* are traditionally carried throughout a community visiting house by house, allowing everyone to be spiritually blessed by the presence of *kami* or to "purify" the communities, though there is not a taboo in Shintoism against touching *omikoshi* as there was in early Judaism (i.e., that the wrath of God would strike down those that touched or mishandled the Ark). In many cases, those that are honored by the opportunity to help carry *omikoshi* undergo a ritual of cleansing and purification not unlike the "sanctification" practices of the Jewish priesthood (1 Chronicles 15:14).

While carrying *omikoshi* around during *matsuri*, those carrying it, and those from the community, call out over and over again "Essa Hoisa, Essa Hoisa" and/or "Wasshoi." These phrases have absolutely no meaning in Japanese, yet have been recited for generations, nonetheless. In Hebrew, however, when those same sounds are pronounced something very different is revealed. In Hebrew "Essa Hoisa, Essa Hoisa" means "lifting up and carrying, lifting up and carrying," and "Wasshoi" means "here comes God." Therefore, when taken together, the whole chant is "Lifting up and carrying, here comes God." Whereas in Japanese the traditional declaration is meaningless, in Hebrew an understandable relationship between the act of carrying the *omikoshi*, or Ark, and the ceremonial purpose thereof is affirmed.

There is a passage in First Chronicles (15:22-28), which provides a description of the Ark as part of Jewish ceremony.

> David and the elders of Israel and the commanders of units of a thousand went to bring up the Ark of the Covenant of the Lord from the house of Obed-Edom, with rejoicing. ...Now David was clothed in the robe of fine linen, as were all the Levites who were carrying the Ark, and as were the singers, and Kenaniah, who was in charge of the singing of the choirs. David also wore a linen ephod. So, all Israel brought up the Ark of the Covenant of the Lord with shouts, with the sounding of rams' horns and trumpets, and of cymbals, and the playing of lyres and harps.

This description would easily fit with the imagery of Shinto festivals and the use of *omikoshi* therein, including the role of singing and musical instruments such as cymbals, drums, etc. Drums and cymbals, for example, are an important part of worship at both *jinja* and in community wide religious ceremonies. The reader may be familiar with *taiko* drums, which were originally a ceremonial feature of Shinto festivals and worship.

There are several key features of the physical make-up of *omikoshi* and what is described in the *Old Testament* as the Ark that are very similar. Atop the Ark of the Covenant the Lord directed that two Cherubim, a sort of winged heavenly angelic figure, be placed and made of gold. *Omikoshi* also have a bird-like figure known as a *hoo*, also made of gold, which is understood to be a heavenly being. The entirety of the Ark was to be overlaid in gold, as are most *omikoshi*, at least they are meant to appear so.

A casual observer to Shinto *matsuri*, festivals or ceremonies of the modern era will find the events are rather commercialized and relatively secular. Very little attention is paid by those in the community to the more traditional aspects of these religious observations. Much like Christmas or Easter festivities among Christian groups, these Shinto ceremonies have become more cultural in nature rather than purely spiritual. The author observed one such *matsuri* in which various districts or neighborhoods of a municipality each competed with each other on the creation of their respective *omikoshi*, including the sound they could make from the drumming and shouting coming from each supporting group. Nevertheless, the basic function and nature of these festivals remain, and give a deeper clue to some fabulous correlations between

Judaism and Shintoism.

On a related note, an eyewitness to the traditions of *omikoshi* at the turn of the nineteenth century, Professor E. Odlum, who had actually spent years traveling around and studying various aspects of Japanese culture and customs, relates another feature of the use of *omikoshi* in ceremony. He states that, though he does not mention in which Shinto ritual, the Ark-like object was carried by priests from a temple down to a river. It was at this point that the priests entered the water just enough to rinse their feet, then turned around and returned to the temple. Prof. Odlum asked what the significance of the practice was and was told that it was simply a tradition passed on from ancient times, and that the true meaning has long since been lost. One cannot, however, as Prof. Odlum did, fail to notice the similarity of this ritual with the story in the *Old Testament* of Joshua descending from Mount Nebo with a cohort of priests carrying the Ark to the river at its base, and subsequently remaining until the last Israelite had passed across the river into Canaan.

Ontousai

As mentioned previously, ritual celebrations, or *matsuri*, are an important component of Shintoism, whether they do or do not resemble the pure or original event. There are literally hundreds of such festivals over the course of a year which vary across the country, city by city in some cases. Some of these events are universally celebrated nationwide such as Obon and Oomatsuri (New Year's) and are not unlike the universality of Christmas and Easter among Christian groups or predominantly Christian nations. Others are more localized and unique to the *kami* of an area. At a passing glance, one may find it difficult to recognize an immediate connection between these events and Judaism. Nonetheless, careful observation reveals an entirely different story.

There is a rather large shrine in Nagano Prefecture on the island of Honshuu at Chino city called Suwa Taisha, and at this *jinja* there is an annual *matsuri* observed on the 15th day of April (March-April when Japan once followed a lunar calendar) called Ontousai. Rising up behind Suwa Taisha is a small mountain called Moriyasan, or Mt. Moriya, and, therefore, the shrine was built to the *kami* believed to dwell there upon. In the ancient past, and according to records, up to at least one hundred and fifty years ago a very sacred and important festival at Suwa Taisha was performed. A young boy from the community was tied by rope to a pillar of wood (*oniya bashira*), and then set in a lying position. A priest then approached the boy while preparing a sharp blade, after which he made a small cut into the pillar. It is at this point that another priest would arrive, and shout in Japanese something like "Do not harm the boy," after which the boy would be subsequently released from his bonds. Could this be a reenactment of the story of Abraham when he nearly sacrificed his son Isaac on Mount Moriah (Moriyyah in Hebrew), or Akeidat Yitzchak, at a recreated location of what was the Temple of Solomon? If not, there is a strange coincidence indeed.

Fig. 28

Fig. 29

Fig. 30 Stone alter on which part of the Ontousai ritual is performed.

Following the above-mentioned portion of the ceremony, seventy-five deer were offered as a sacrifice to
the *kami*; a ritual called *miisakuchi* (mi-isaku-chi). Animal sacrifice, too, is consistent with what happened in
the Biblical account of Abraham and Isaac after the an-

gel asked Abraham to release Isaac. The angel declared that Abraham should make an offering to the Lord. While Abraham made an offering of a first-born ram, perhaps deer were substituted in Japan since ram are not native to the islands. Deer, as it turns out, are *kosher* under Jewish dietary law, and would have been a perfectly acceptable substitute. It should be noted that animal sacrifice is not an associated practice of Shintoism in recent historical memory. However, animal sacrifice would have been part of the ancient cultures of the islands such as the Ainu, who, it will be argued later, are the true descendants of the Lost Tribes of Israel. It is more likely that it is not that Shintoism discouraged or discourages animal sacrifice, but that the Buddhist preference for vegetarianism and protection of all living creatures became a syncretic influence over time on early Shintoism.

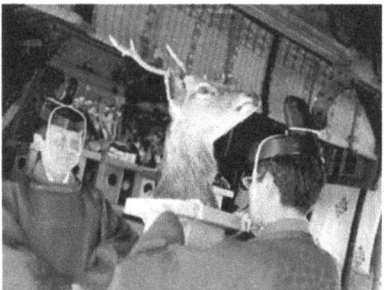

Fig. 31

Today, the ceremony is consistently performed year after year, but without ritually tying a boy to a pole, or the sacrificial deer. During the Meiji Era, there was a public backlash against the act of tying a boy to the ceremonial pillar, and the deer were eventually replaced with stuffed animals. There is, however, still a pillar involved, which is called *oniya bashira*, or sacrifice pillar. This portion of the overall festival is called Oniyabashia-sai, which takes place once every seven years, and involves bringing a set of cypress pillars down from the top of a mountain in order to replace the older existing ones. It is believed that spirits, referred to specifically as *hashira*, dwell in the pillars. This belief is interestingly similar to the ancient Jewish belief that the Goddess Asherah was somehow connected to the cypress logs brought down from Mount Lebanon every seven years. Even the Japanese term for these supposed spirits, *hashira*, sounds the same as the Canaanite Goddess Asherah.

Tama *matsuri* and *Juugoya*

Another important date on the lunar calendar for ancient Japan was the fifteenth day of the seventh month. This day corresponded with Tama *matsuri*. It was a harvest feast of sorts. The fifteenth day of the seventh month also happens to be the day on which ancient Judaism celebrated the Feast of the Booths, before it was changed to the fifteenth day of the eighth month by King Jeroboam. The Feast of the Booths, too, is a harvest feast. In fact, the Jewish Feast of the Booths was the remnant of a ritual associated with Baal, which helps support the notion that even in early Judaism other cultic worship still had its lingering places within the greater pantheon.

What makes the celebration of Tama *matsuri* unique is the specific traditions of singing and dancing. At Tama *matsuri* in ancient times, specifically single men and women would gather to sing and dance (*utagaki*), with the purpose of finding a mate and getting engaged. This was a similar tradition for the Jewish Feast of Booths. From the period of the introduction of Buddhism in Japan, and the subsequent syncretization with Shintoism, Tama *mastsuri* was eventually replaced by a Buddhist holiday known as Obon. The traditions of Tama *matsuri* were stripped away over time and overshadowed by those of Obon.

Tama *matsuri*, or the celebrations on the fifteenth day of the seventh month, are also related to another custom called *juugoya*. It is the *juugoya* tradition, connected to this feast day, that most closely corresponds to the Feast of Booths festival of ancient Judaism. As part of the harvest festival, families gather together with the other families of the community to each build a booth and make an offering of the first fruits of their harvest at the shrine in recognition of the role that the *kami* played in bringing it forth. This tradition of offering the first fruits to a deity is also a strong part of the Jewish faith from ancient times, in which first fruits were presented to God on little booths at the Tabernacle in the desert originally, and at Solomon's Temple later on (Exodus 34:26).

In the Jewish tradition, the first fruit offerings were gathered from among the numerous booths and brought to the temple priests. The priests then conducted a separate and private ceremony of presenting the collective offerings to the Lord before feasting on those offerings "in the presence of the Lord." In similar fashion, there is a private ceremony called Niinamesai which is performed by the emperor of Japan (think priestly king) or high priests. After the first fruits of *juugoya* have been gathered, the offerings accepted, and then presented to *kami*, they proceed to feast on the offerings supposedly in the presence of *kami*. It is interesting to note that the emperors of Japan traditionally ascended to the throne in a ceremony held on the fifteenth day of the seventh month. They participated in a private feast after they had ascended the throne known as the Daijousai, which is essentially a special Niinamesai feast, but representative of the added importance of the day.

Weddings (*Kekkonshiki*)

Wedding ceremonies are one of the most recognizable sacramental functions of any culture. However, most weddings that take place today share a very Christianized and Westernized recipe, with very little variation. One can travel between India to Ireland, Japan to Canada, Peru to China, and most people in this modern era choose the more Western standard of ceremony. Wedding rites were, nevertheless, much more culturally diverse and nuanced in the ancient world. Each ceremony would have been a strict extension of the unique religious codes and beliefs of each people. This was definitely the case with both Judaism and Shintoism, and there are several clear similarities worth noting between these two faiths.

In the traditional Shinto wedding ceremony, the bride and groom partake of *sake* (rice wine) from the same glass. In the same fashion, Jewish brides and grooms drink from the same cup of wine. It is interesting to note that after this part of the ceremony in the Jewish custom the groom places the empty wine glass on the ground and breaks it, symbolizing the destruction of the Temple. This part of the wedding ritual was introduced sometime after the destruction of the last temple. This custom does not exist in the Shinto ceremony. If the Japanese people, and the Shinto faith, are descended from the Lost Tribes of Israel, who were forced to leave the Holy Land approximately eight hundred years before the destruction of the last temple, the absence of glass breaking in Shintoism could be explained.

For the early form of the Shinto wedding the bride wore a shawl or covering, called a *kazuki*, which would cover the whole face, and this was also worn when attending a shrine. This has been the custom in Jewish weddings going back to at least the prophet Jacob's time, when, according to the *Bible*, he was deceived into marrying Lear, his bride Rachel's sister, because he did not know who was under the wedding veil. It is also the case that women, at least in ancient times, were required to wear a shawl when going to synagogue.

For Shinto wedding rituals, it is required that the priest officiating the ceremony be married. It is similarly the case that in ancient times, Jewish priests conducting weddings had to be married. On a slightly related note, in early Judaism it was the custom that if a woman's husband passed away, and the husband had an unmarried brother, the woman was married to the brother. This was also a common practice in early Japan, though it began dying out during the Meiji period, just as it did among practicing Jews.

Dedication of Horses to the Sun

Horses have always played an important part for many early peoples dating back as far as pre-historic times, whether for practical or spiritual reasons. Horses have been depicted on cave walls by early hominids, worshiped, and even, in the case of Shintoism and Judaism, used for ritualistic dedication offerings to the Sun.

In ancient Japan there were many shrines, such as is still the case at Ise Grand Shrine, at which horses were ritualistically dedicated to the sun Goddess Amaterasu.

At some point this practice became unsustainable, and was replaced by offering paintings of horses, called *ema*. These *ema*, plates of wood on which the image of a horse is painted, and words of prayers written, can be found posted up at shrines. The dedication of horses to the sun was also a ritual of ancient Israel, and mentioned in 2 Kings 23:11, in which King Josiah, in an effort to reform the faith, is described as removing the horses from the Temple that had been dedicated to the sun. This custom was closely connected with the cult of Baal, a tradition of sun worship of the sun god Baal. The cult of Baal is mentioned numerous times in the *Old Testament* as being an abomination and attempts were made on several occasions to remove such worship from Israel. The worship of Baal, a tradition that was part of the greater spiritual pantheon of nearly all Semitic peoples, including the Canaanites, prior to the transition of mono-lateralism from the time of Abraham, would have still been important to nearly all other cultures of the region. Therefore, it is entirely possible that the exiled Israelites blended aspects of the varying cultic worship of Baal freely with Judaism and carried that syncretization with them on the further migrations eastward.

The Rite of Passage into Adulthood

The transition from childhood to adulthood is an important milestone in the life of every person. So much so that numerous cultures from ancient times right up to today have marked this period with elaborate celebrations, rituals, or other such ceremonies. These rituals are meant to symbolize a child's growth into a young adult, with all of the responsibilities and duties that accompany adulthood, be they religious, familial, or within the community. Judaism is probably the one religion most notable for its rites of passage, celebrating the *Bar Mitzvah* for young men and *Bat Mitzvah* for young women.

The ceremony, or *mitzvah*, of a boy entering manhood is not mentioned in the *Bible*, and the first time it is mentioned in a written record is around the third century CE. However, it is likely an older custom. In the Jewish faith, when a boy turns thirteen years of age he participates in a set of rituals to celebrate his passing into manhood. It also marks the point from which he becomes fully responsible for his personal commitment and relationship with God.

There was just such a ceremony in early Shintoism called *Genpukushiki* in which a boy of thirteen would attend a shrine with his family. He entered the *jinja* wearing adult clothes and received a blessing for his adulthood. It was also traditional that the name the child had in boyhood would be replaced with one for adulthood.

Gion Festival

Another very well-known Shinto festival, traditionally held on the seventeenth day of the seventh month of the lunar calendar, is the Gion *matsuri*. While the Gion *matsuri* is performed today at numerous shrines throughout Japan, the original celebration took place at the Gion *jinja* in Kyoto, and in its ancient form was held over an eight-day period. The day of this Shinto event just so happens to coincide with the supposed day on which the *Bible* describes Noah's Ark coming to rest on top of Mount Ararat (Genesis 8:4). It should be noted that the Gion festival traditionally begins with the participants chanting "En yalah yah," a phrase which has absolutely no meaning in Japanese. However, the phrase has significant meaning when phonetically converting it into Hebrew as "eni ahalel yah," which means "I praise Yahweh." Could the Gion *matsuri* be the remnant of an ancient Jewish festival of remembrance of Noah's family being able to depart safely from the Ark? Could the opening chant symbolize the praise and prayer Noah might have offered to the Lord upon living safely through the deluge? The Feast of the Booths, which was held two days earlier, has since taken precedence, though there are some shrines that still hold the Gion festival.

As part of the overall Gion festival, like most other Shinto festivals, *omikoshi* arks are guided through towns, villages, and city streets. In Kyoto, the Gion festival showcases extraordinarily large *omikoshi*. That, however, is not anything unusual. What does make them unusual is the images draped over the sides of them. Many of these floats bear images depicting the Israelites' exodus from Egypt with the Pyramids in the background, cityscapes of Babylon, and caravans moving across the Silk Roads. Remarkably, one scene appears to show the Biblical story of Rebecca presenting a servant of Abraham with water (Genesis 24). The director of the Gion festival floats association was interviewed by an NHK (Japanese national broadcaster) television program around the year 2007 about why these floats, or *omikoshi*, displayed this imagery. His response was very matter of fact. It was, as he explained, because the origins of the whole festival were rooted in a Jewish ancestry.

Fig. 32

Fig. 33

Fig. 34

It is worth noting at this point that the more precise place in which it is believed Noah's Ark came to rest is at Togarmah, Armenia. The "arme" of the Armenia means "heaven," and the "nia" means "place of." The ancient Japanese believed that they were descended from a place called Takamagahara, which means "Plain of High Heaven." There is a similarity in both the sounds of these two place names as well as in meaning.

The Sabbath

Another of the more recognizable and widely known rituals characteristic of Judaism, and part of the entire Judeo-Christo-Islamic traditions more broadly, is that of Sabbath worship. Unlike some other important features of Judaism that were added or evolved later such as Passover, the Sabbath is one of the original aspects of the Abrahamic Covenant, or part of proto-Judaism. The Jewish observance of the Sabbath begins at sunset on the sixth day of the week until sunset on the seventh day of the week. For most of the modern era this has been from sunset on Friday evening until sunset on Saturday evening. There is a long list of restrictions that coincide with the observances required of Jews during this roughly twenty-four-hour period (affected by geography). The only other known faith to have such traditions so closely resembling this is Islam, in its various forms and syncretizations, including Sikhism. Or is it?

There is a long-standing tradition in Japan that portions of society called the *eta hinin*, or filthy non-humans, in and around the Nagasaki prefecture had practiced a peculiarly unique weekly ceremony called Sabato Yori. Sabato Yori means "gathering of Sabato." The term sabato, however, has no meaning or translation in Japanese, and is undeniably similar to the Hebrew for "sabbath," or *shabbath*. The *eta hinin*, also referred to as *burakumin*, meaning "hamlet people" (similar to the unkind epithet "redneck"), were the lowest possible caste within Japan's very strictly regimented social hierarchy. They were considered the dredge of the dredge. How did a destitute class of people in ancient Japan come to practice a day or worship remarkably similar to the Sabbath of Judaism? The answer may lie in the possible origins of those of this caste.

The origins of the *eta hinin* are not entirely clear in any historical record. How did certain people among the island's many inhabitants find themselves a part of this social station? Were they purposely outcast? If so, for what reasons? While these questions may not have any answers within historical or oral traditions, there are some other clues that may help. From the time that the more Asiatic, or Koreanic, peoples from the mainland began settling on the islands of Japan, around 300 BCE, or what is the transition point from the Yayoi to Yamato Periods, those Asiatic migrants began and continued a pattern of ethnic persecution to varying levels of severity of the older inhabitants of the islands such as the Ainu and other groups, as mentioned elsewhere. It is known that the Asiatic population of the islands, which very quickly dominated all aspects of life in Japan, and continue to do so to this day, refused to accept the early races on the islands within society as a whole, forcing them, rather, to live on the fringes of existence in every sense of the idea. Could the term *eta hinin* be referring to the non-Asiatic peoples of Japan, and their status as unwanted and eventually destitute within greater society? Since it will be argued later that the Ainu are perhaps the descendants of the Ten Lost Tribes of Israel, could this be another example of what has become a global phenomenon of Jewish persecution? If so, then it would possibly explain why a group within Japanese society practiced and observed the Sabbath. It is also possible that these Asiatic migrants are the second wave of Israelite exiles from the Second Exile that may have assimilated much more with cultures and peoples among whom they settled on their own journey eastward.

Some have argued against this evidence by bringing up the fact that Christian missionaries and traders, who began arriving in ports of Japan such as Nagasaki in the late 1500's CE, were introducing their faith to the Japanese, and in the process finding some converts. These same critics state that it is logical to assume that the most marginalized of Japanese society could have found comfort in the message of this new, foreign, faith, like those among the *eta hinin*, for example, believing it to be a message of "hope." Therefore, and according to this line of thought, the reason for the tradition of "sabbath worship" among the *eta hinin* is related to the adoption of Christianity, and not as a lingering tradition of ancient times. This is entirely possible.

Two important observations, however, do need to be mentioned as points of contention. The first is that while Christianity has a tradition of Sabbath worship, as described in the New Testament, it is ritualistically quite distinct from the *Old Testament* understanding of the practice. In fact, aside from using the term "sabbath," and the observance of setting one day aside a week for spiritual reflection, there is virtually nothing concretely connecting the two observances. Secondly, the first Christian missionaries to Japan were Catholic priests of the Jesuit order. This was one of several Catholic orders which were active in Europe during the fourteenth to sixteenth centuries, purging Western Europe of what they claimed to be "heretics" but were nothing more than non-Catholics. One such group that Jesuits chased out of Western Europe were the Jews. Therefore, it is highly unlikely that the Jesuit priestly missionaries, these very devout Catholic men that followed a very rigid form of their faith, were introducing Jewish traditions to the Japanese. It is more likely, then, that the *eta hinin*, as reported in interviews during the Meiji Era, had been practicing this worship observance which was similar to the Jewish Sabbath from even before the arrival of Europeans.

Lunar New Year Celebration

Early Japan, like most cultures of the ancient past, including Semitic peoples like the Israelites, based their calendar on the cycles of the moon, a lunar calendar. In fact, it was not until the Meiji period, and the Westernization and modernization of the administrations of that period, that Japan began to use the solar calendar. Therefore, New Year's is recognized today as January 1 of each year as with the rest of the Westernized world. However, Lunar New Year for early Japan once fell upon the fifteenth day of the first lunar month because it was the first full moon of the new year. For the Israelites, observance of Passover, and the Passover Feast, became the event that helped marked their new year.

On the first day of the Lunar New Year (now January 1 every year) the Japanese of the past would partake of a type of porridge made with seven bitter herbs. It was, and still is, customary for families to gather together on the first day of the year for a feast, and it is frowned upon to do any work or labor of any kind on this day. Japan literally shuts down on New Year's with very few exceptions, even in this modern era. A set of special food called *osechi ryori* is consumed for the occasion of the New Year's feast, all of which is prepared or purchased before midnight on the last day of the previous year. A whole catering industry exists now in Japan for families that would rather order their New Year's meal and have it delivered before New Year's Day rather than prepare it themselves. Over the first seven days after New Year's Day, it is tradition in Japan to eat a type of sticky rice ball called *mochi*. Similarly, Jews follow a practice of eating unleavened bread, or *matzah*, for the first seven days after Lunar New Year. The recipe and purpose of *matzah* and *mochi* are quite similar. It is also upon the transition from one year to another that the Japanese have the custom of cleaning their homes thoroughly, as well as purging their homes of unnecessary things, known as *osouji*.

All of these traditions and customs closely relate to the Jewish Passover Feast, or Feast of Unleavened Bread, and the practices before and after that feast day. Passover, the ritualistic day of remembrance for the Jewish faithful of the evening prior to being initially granted escape from Egypt and saved from the supposed Angel of Death taking the lives of the first born of the families that had marked their doors' thresholds with the blood of a first-born ram. Hence the name Passover because the Angel of Death passed over their homes. The Jewish community was commanded by Moses to prepare unleavened bread, among other food that could be readied quickly for their anticipated long journey out of Egypt. This custom continues as part of this yearly Passover Feast, during which families eat a meal which was prepared prior to Passover. As with the Japanese New Year's Day, it is also part of the Jewish belief that no work or labor be done on Passover. It is supposed to be a day of sacrament. Also, like the Japanese, Jews engage in thorough cleaning of their homes on New Year's Eve as described in Exodus 12:15.

On a related note, there was a practice among the early peoples of the Ryukyu islanders (the southernmost collection of Japanese islets) that has a remarkable connection to the Passover customs described in the *Bible*. Essentially, communities would slaughter a first-born calf (sheep would not have been found) and smear the blood of the cow using a bundle of grass or mulberry leaves on the thresholds of homes and other buildings. It is said that the purpose of performing this act was to keep out evil and prevent other negative things from entering. This ritual is called *kanka* (to be overlooked) or *shimaku-sarashi* (to drive away).

Offerings

Every religion, ancient or contemporary, seems to have some set principles or protocols for making sacrifices or offerings, whether those offerings are presented to a deity or deities, or for the general benefit of the clergy and administrative expenses. Judaism and Shintoism, as already stated, are no exceptions. Offerings, sacrifices, or tithes – whatever form these obligations may take, the practice plays an important role in the overall worship-fulness of the body of believers, a physical act or symbolic way that the body of the faithful show gratitude and recognition.

In Shintoism, there are three types of offerings made: an offering of rice or *mochi* (a grain), *sake* (a liquor), and a burnt offering (incense). These offerings can be presented to a *kami* at a shrine at any time, but usually on feast (*matsuri*) days or at the family shrine within the home. Traditionally these offerings were to be the first fruits of a harvest or slaughtering, for example, but nowadays almost anything is acceptable – one of the many ways Buddhism has influenced Shintoism. It is still the case today, as in ancient times, that offerings made at the shrine are gathered by the priests and placed on a table made of wood inside the Holy Place (*haidan*). A priest then says a prayer to the *kami*, offering up the gifts. After which, the priests partake of the offerings in the Holy Place, in the presence of the *kami*.

A description of the Shinto practice of making offerings

at *jinja*, and the sacred rituals thereafter performed by the priesthood at the shrines would be quite recognizable to anyone familiar with what is presented in the *Old Testament*. There would have been very little difference found in early Judaism. During the time of the Tabernacle, and lasting until the second temple was destroyed, it was also the practice of Jews to present their first fruits to the Lord, on feast days or otherwise. These were usually unleavened bread (*matzah*), wine, and a burnt offering of a lamb. Those offerings were gathered up by the priests and placed upon a wooden table inside the Holy Place. A priest would pray to the Lord on behalf of those that made the offerings and present them to Him, asking Him to accept the offerings. After this ritual was performed, it was the custom for the priests of the Tabernacle/Temple to consume the offerings with their families.

It should be noted that there was a tradition among the Ainu people of worshiping the deity of cereals or grains. Part of this worship was making *mochi*, or cooked rice pounded into little balls, with grain from the first rice harvest of the year. Before consuming *mochi*, the priests and worshipers recited a prayer of thanksgiving:

> O thou cereal deity, we worship thee. Thou hast grown very well this year, and thy flavor will be sweet. Thou art good. The goddess of fire will be glad, and we also shall rejoice greatly. O thou god, O thou divine cereal, do thou nourish the people. I now partake of thee. I worship thee and give thanks.

After offering a prayer, the priests and congregants consumed the *mochi*. Could this annual ceremony of the

114

Ainu be the remnant of the First Fruits offerings of Jews at the Tabernacle or Temple, or at home shrines?

Physical Appearance

Mizura and *Peyot*

In ancient Japan, approximately before the fifth century CE, based on artifacts found depicting *samurai* of that early period, there was a popular way in which men of the *samurai* class wore their hair. The custom of having curled locks of hair hanging down from underneath their skull caps in front of the ears was called *mizura*. While much of the fashion, art, and architecture of early Japan was influenced by dynastic China, this hair fashion was unique to Japan.

Fig. 35 – Statuette of a samurai warrior from around the 5ᵗʰ Century CE

There is a great deal of similarity, visually, between the

mizura worn by men of the *samurai* class of ancient Japan and the custom in Judaism, both ancient and contemporary, of wearing their hair in a similar fashion; locks of curled hair hanging down in front of the ears. This custom in Judaism is known as *peyot* (Leviticus 19:27).

Fig. 36 – Jewish boys wearing their hair in a peyot.

Was there a reason for this similar custom or is it a mere coincidence?

Facial Hair

Like many of the ancient Semitic peoples of western Asia, the Ainu (see Chapter 11 for a full evaluation of the Ainu connection to the Lost Tribes of Israel) also placed great importance on the beards of men. The Ainu considered male facial hair a sign of strength, virility, manhood, and good looks. This was the case in ancient Israel, as illustrated in 2 Samuel 10. To remove the beard of a man, or force him to remove it, was one of the cruelest ways to shame, defile, or otherwise, punish that man.

116

Beliefs of Impurity and Ritualistic Cleansing

Having a belief in the importance of the purification of body, spirit, and place, along with an understanding of what constitutes what is or is not impure, is common among ancient and contemporary belief systems alike. However, very few have such broad and rigid sets of guidance as is found in Judaism. Shintoism, it will be described, has a remarkably similar set of ideas.

Bathing Rituals

Every Jewish community, from ancient times to present, has had what is called a *mikveh*, or bath house. It is at a *mikveh* that members of the Jewish community would periodically go to ritualistically cleanse themselves. The fact that communities had communal bath houses is of little importance. It is the protocols of these *mikveh*, nevertheless, that must be emphasized. Firstly, males and females adjourn into two separate halves of the *mikveh*. Women that are menstruating may not enter. Non-Jews are not allowed in. Girls and boys that have not reached adulthood cannot enter either. Upon entering the baths, one must first purify themselves by washing the body. Only after having completely washed may one enter the bath for cleansing.

This process of cleaning oneself is nearly the same as the custom in early Japan. Nowadays bath houses in Japan, largely in an effort to not become obsolete, are catering more and more to the whims of their clientele, with sections for whole families to gather privately, the acceptance of foreigners there, and other such accommodations. Nonetheless, the customs of the bath houses in early Japan were quite clear. Both genders were separated and menstruating women and adolescents that had not yet reached adulthood were not allowed. Foreigners traditionally were not allowed in or had a certain time during which they could bath or had their own separate bath houses. The process of bathing was, and still is, precisely the same as in the Jewish custom; people must thoroughly shower first before entering the bath.

This two-step cleaning ritual, it must be noted, is the same today, whether for Jews or Japanese, when going to a bathhouse or at home. Most Japanese homes are designed with bathrooms that accommodate this, though that is changing in some cases. It should also be pointed out that the outbreak of plagues in the ancient world affected Jewish and Japanese populations much less than they did other peoples. Shinto and Levite priests both were, and in Shintoism still are, required to ritualistically wash their hands and mouths prior to entering the holy sanctuaries or performing any religious obligation. Additionally, the priestly garb worn by the priests in both traditions had to also be newly cleaned in freshwater.

Sanctification with Water and Salt

As with bathing rituals, fresh water is believed by both Jews and adherents to Shintoism, past and present, to have special properties which allow for one to be purified or cleansed. Not only are lay believers required to follow certain customs when bathing regularly, Jewish and Shinto priests are expected to ceremonially wash their clothes and bathe in fresh water prior to fulfilling their sacred duties within their respective sanctuaries. This may be why sources of fresh water were and are often found at the sites of Shinto shrines, or why oasis and sources of water were so critical to early Western Asian peoples like the Hebrews.

But water is for the purification of man (*misogi*). Salt was, and still is, used to sanctify objects or places. In the Shinto tradition salt is placed at the site of new construction, along with being blessed and consecrated in some cases by Shinto priests. Salt is often placed at the entrance of homes or businesses. *Sumo* wrestlers sprinkle salt in an elaborate ceremony at the beginning of each bout as a way of sanctifying the ring in which they will compete. Salt also plays an important part within certain purification rituals in Judaism, though, perhaps not as it once was. Nevertheless, it is still relatively common for Jews to welcome guests to their homes, or the entrance to their cities, with an offering of salt and *hallah* (yeast-leavened bread). Part of the process of preparing *kosher* meat is salting the meat in order to absorb the blood. Salt is also part of the process of making offerings at every religious festival in both faiths (Leviticus 2:13). Salt is one of the more common items given as sacrifices at Shinto shrines, as it was at the early Jewish Tabernacle or later Temples. Prior to the Meiji era, apparently, and in early Judaism as described in the *Old Testament*, salt was rubbed on newborn babies prior to bathing the babies for the first time. This was done as a kind of sanctification of children for the beginning of their lives, and very similar in meaning and symbolism as baptisms in Christianity.

It is interesting to note that, for the Jews, salt was understood to be the antithesis of decay and death and was considered symbolic of the eternal covenant a Jew makes with the Lord. In a similar fashion, salt was used and believed to have the same spiritual role and meaning in the Egyptian religious traditions, perhaps because of its vital role in the mummification process. Could the importance of salt have been passed from Egypt on to the Israelites, and therefore, to Shintoism?

The Unclean Dead

Related to the similarities between Shintoism and Judaism with respect to the use of that mineral in various purification rites, salt is also used in Shintoism when a person "cleanses" themselves after having touched a dead body or returning from funerary services. This was considered a pollutant, or *kegare*, or the soul. Shintoism and Judaism both prescribe a very specific rite that must be performed after touching a deceased individual or after attending a funeral. What connects these two faiths is not that salt is used in both cleansing rituals, but that there is a very clear purification process adherents to both faiths must follow in the case of death. However, fresh water, whether sprinkled or as a bath, is used. On a related note, a person that has had contact with a dead body, or has attended a funeral ceremony, is considered unclean for a certain number of days. In Judaism that period lasts for seven days. In Shintoism, a person may not attend a shrine or other religious ceremony, and in ancient Israel a person could not go to the Tabernacle or Temple or religious festival. For the very reason that death and "uncleanliness" were and are believed to go hand-in-hand, funeral services in both Judaism and Shintoism are never conducted on the site of a shrine and are always conducted outside of a shrine complex.

John Batchelor recounts in his 1901 publication about the Ainu people, and his experience living with them for a time, that when he returned to the home of his host family after a funeral service, the women brought him a bowl of fresh water to wash himself. While doing so, the women also brushed him down with a bundle of grass. It was explained to him that this ritual would chase away disease, evil spirits, or other harmful things he may have brought back with him from the presence of the dead.

Menstruation and Childbirth

Since ancient times, the early inhabitants of the islands of Japan have had a very distinct set of protocols and norms as related to women during menstruation and childbirth. Many of these practices lasted well into the Meiji era, and, therefore, are still very much part of the collective memory. Women were not allowed to participate in any Shinto festival or to visit a community shrine or make offerings during menstruation. They were not, consequently, allowed to worship before the shrine at home or make offerings there either. Sexual intercourse was also forbidden between a husband and wife during the menstrual period and a wife was expected to remain isolated for a period of seven days. In fact, women were expected to remain isolated in a special hut referred to as a *gekkei-goya*. These restrictions were assumed necessary because it was believed that women were "unclean" during their menstrual period. Thusly, when the seven-day period of isolation was over, a woman was expected to bathe herself in a natural body of water where possible, or in an *onsen* supplied by natural water.

These very strict limitations placed on women in ancient Japanese society during this particular time for a woman are almost entirely the same as imposed by Judaism. Within the Jewish traditional understanding of "cleanliness" women were also not allowed to attend holy functions of any kind, touch or make offerings, have sexual relations with their husbands, and were also isolated in a separate place for a period of seven days. It was, and still is, believed that this period of isolation was part of the cleansing process, or ritual purification. When a Jewish woman's menstruation has ended, and the seven-day period of isolation is over, she enters the *mikvah*, or ritual bath. The water used in a *mikvah*, according to Jewish law, must be natural water (rainwater counts).

Similarly, childbirth is another period during which both Shintoism and Judaism have the belief that women are "unclean" or "impure." According to very old Japanese customs, and as is the case with Judaism, a woman may not participate in any holy events or festivals for a seven-day period from the moment of childbirth. The exception to this similarity between these two faiths is that early Judaism, as outlined in the *Bible*, stipulated a further period of "purification" of thirty-three days in the case of the birth of a male, and sixty-six additional days for that of a female. Whereas in Shintoism a woman must only wait an additional thirty-one days after the birth of a male child and thirty-three for a female. Nevertheless, it is only after this prolonged period of waiting that a mother may take her child to the shrine, in the case of Shintoism.

The Ainu had a custom whereby women must remain isolated in a separate hut in their respective villages for seven days. On the seventh day they were allowed to emerge but were required to first cleanse themselves in a body of fresh water. Until such time women were not allowed to rejoin society. This ritual of purification was called roro-oshiraya. Is this cleansing process, after which a woman may resume daily duties within the home or approach their god, part of the overall heritage brought to Japan by the Ainu people, and are the Ainu in actuality remnants of the Lost Tribes of Israel (see Chapter 11)?

Oshichiya (Remnants of the Celebration of Circumcision)

Circumcision, or the ritual removal of the foreskin of the male reproductive organ, was first widely practiced from the Abrahamic era by, according to the *Old Testament*, those that made a covenant or promise to the god of Abraham. It was a physical symbol meant to represent that spiritual commitment. It is believed that circumcision was unique to Judaism, and later some sects of Christianity, and even later, Islam. Today, circumcision is still popular in many parts of the world, though parents are usually given the choice.

From the time of Abraham, it has been the custom that male children be circumcised on the eighth day of life. This rite is referred to as *brit milah*, or more commonly as a *bris*. The *brit milah* takes place on the eighth day of life no matter what day on which it falls. This is important because this allows the mother to finish her seven-day period of impurity. *Bris* are either conducted at synagogue or in the family home, and are overseen by men (*mohel*), and in some cases women (*mohelet*), that have been trained under Jewish law. In addition to performing a circumcision, the ceremony also coincides with the male child receiving his Hebrew name, which in some cases, is also his given name, and a blessing on the child. Female children also have a special ritual on their eighth day of life, called *brit banot*. While a circumcision is not performed, a blessing is also given in which

123

the female child is "brought" into a covenant with God. *Brit banot* are a more recent development, however, and meant to be more inclusive. In the case of both rituals, participants wrap up the celebrations with a special feast known as *shalom zakhar*.

There is virtually no other religious tradition with a rite of passage for children like the *brit milah* or *brit banot*, with the exception of Shintoism. From ancient times, the Japanese had a Shinto rite of passage for children called *oshichiya*, or Seventh Night. On the seventh night after the day of birth, or, in other words, the night of the eighth day of birth, the family of a newborn child gathered for a feast, and to officially name the child. As already mentioned, this also coincides with the day after a mother has passed out of her impure period after childbirth according to Japanese tradition. The major difference between *brit milah* and *oshichiya* is that the Japanese do not have a tradition of circumcision. Could *oschichiya* be a long since morphed form of *brit milah* that lost the original intent of the rite?

Lack of Idol Worship

The *Old Testament*, from the story of Abraham forward, is replete with references to the prohibition handed down by the Jewish god to the people against creating or worshiping any form of idol or manmade image. This law of the cult of Yahweh is of course made famous with the story of Moses' ascension to Mount Sinai in order to receive revelation from God, and subsequently, and supposedly, destroying a golden calf that the Israelites had made and were worshiping while he was away. The god of the Jews made it abundantly clear, according to the *Old Testament*, through the voices of numerous prophets that He was to be the only being they worshiped, but that even He should not have idols made of him for the purpose of worship.

Shintoism is another system of faith, as with the cult of Yahweh, in which the creation and worship of idols, statues, or other such manmade imagery of deities does not exist. Virtually all religious traditions, institutionalized or not, with the exception of several belief systems that originated in Southwest Asia such as Judaism, Zoroastrianism, Christianity, and Islam, have some form of worship of idols. Shintoism is, therefore, and for many reasons, a spiritual island, as is Japan, on the edge of Asia. And, despite the heavy influence of Buddhism, and tremendous pressure to conform over the past fourteen or fifteen hundred years, Shintoism never adopted the statue worshiping component that Buddhism adopted early in its own history. When one enters a Shinto *jinja*, stands in front of a home shrine, or a sacred grove, no images or manmade objects for worship will be found.

Pillars of Stone

One of the lesser known, and largely forgotten artifacts of worship of the ancient Israelites is the creation of pillars of stone, which were believed to be representative of God (Genesis 35:14).

> "...Jacob set up a pillar of stone in a sacred area, and he called the name of the place where God spoke to him Beth-El."

These megalithic stone structures predate the Tabernacle or temples. Offerings were once made at these pillars of a fermented drink. According to the *Old Testament*, Moses had twelve such pillars erected, one for each tribe of Israel (Exodus 24:4). King Saul, the first king of Israel, is even referenced to have created such an altar of natural, "unhewn" stone for the purpose of worship. Saul arguably used a stone that was unaltered because of the Jewish law prohibiting the carving of stone for use in sacred spaces (Exodus 20:25). Over time, however, these pillars of stone came to be associated with idol worship among the early Israelites, and several prophets condemned the inclusion of the pillars in worship (1 Kings 14:23). Thus, the role that these formerly sacred sites played in Judaism is little known or understood by contemporary Jews, and those that have heard of them associate them with idol worship or paganism.

Interestingly enough, there are remarkably similar stone monuments or pillars found in several places in Japan, notably in Akita and Ibaraki prefectures. These pillars are regarded to be sacred stones from ancient times and built to be places of or for the gods – the very places where the gods would come to sit and rest according to the mythology. These stones are, as in Israel, of unhewn stone because, and again, as with Jewish law, stonework used in Shinto sacred spaces is to be unaltered. And just as Jacob, Saul, and other leaders of Israel supposedly made sacrifices of fermented drink at these altars, so too did Shinto priests offer *sake*, such as at the stone pillars now found to the rear of Kashima shrine.

Could the role of these stone pillars in an earlier form of Judaism, before the importance of such sites was discouraged, have passed from the land of Israel to the island of Japan by descendants of the Lost Tribes of Israel? Interestingly, the Japanese records mention that the *kami*

Izanagi and Izanami, the offspring of the goddess Ama-terasu, when wed, performed a ceremony around the base of a pillar, while chanting "ana-niyasi." This phrase, however, has no meaning in Japanese. When converted phonetically, though, into Hebrew-Aramaic, as "ana-ni-sa," we get the exclamation "I wed." Even today, Jewish brides circle their groom in wedding ceremonies. Is this practice a remnant of a much earlier symbolic gesture familiar in both cultures?

Fig. 37 – Twelve standing stones at the base of Mount Karkom

Fig. 38 – Stone pillars found at Kabayama, Japan

Daily Priestly Prayer

Prayer is not a unique feature to Shintoism or Judaism, as it would be hard pressed to find any spiritual tradition without some facet resembling prayer. Therefore, prayer alone is not evidence of a connection between Judaism and Shintoism. Nevertheless, the resemblance between those respective prayer practices of the priesthoods can be considered. Shinto priests rise early each day before sunrise in order to be positioned, kneeling, facing east, in order to welcome the rising sun with prayer. This is very similar to the practice of Jewish priests of the First Temple in Jerusalem.

> They would blow (the horn) and would walk until the gate which went out to the east. They would turn their faces (from the east) to the west and proclaim: "When our fathers were in this place, their backs were to the Temple courtyard and their faces to the east, and they would bow down to the east and the sun, whereas our eyes are turned to the Eternal."

Sumo

One of the most iconic cultural features of Japan, and almost universally ubiquitous with that culture, is the wrestling sport known as *sumo*. Stylistically it is quite unique from other forms of wrestling passed down from the ancient world, such as Greco-Roman. Even non-Japanese could recognize and identify some of the more pronounced characteristics of this sport. In an almost ritualistic manner, two men, usually quite large, wait reverently outside of the wrestling circle while the referee, dressed more like a Shinto priest, chants a prayer. Before entering the circular space, the two men toss a handful of salt about as a gesture of sanctifying and purifying the ring. After the opening honorifics, the two combatants enter the sacred space in which they will compete and begin to go through a series of stretches and other protocols to prepare themselves for the contest. Essentially, whichever combatant can push their opponent out of the ring or cause their opponent to fall first wins. The victor is nowadays rewarded with money, but they were once rewarded with rice. Women are not allowed to compete, and until very recently, were not even allowed to be a spectator.

In the ancient traditions, *sumo* wrestlers were believed to possess the strength of the gods, because it was understood that they were gods or demigods themselves. Therefore, this was combat between one god/demigod with another. Even today, *sumo* wrestlers command great respect and honor. But was this practice of ancient Israelite origins? According to the head of the Yoshida-tsukasa clan in Kumamoto Prefecture, the clan which, for eight hundred years until 1949, was charged by the emperor to maintain and preserve *sumo*, was originally of the Shinto faith. This was, therefore, very much a Shinto ritual, and thus a connection to gods. The original form of that ritualistic battle was believed to have been the symbolic act of battle with a god, or *kami*, for blessings for mankind. Kubo Arimasa, one of the leading figures on the study of the correlations between ancient Japan and Israel, states that the very term *sumo* is in fact of Hebrew-Aramaic origins, or the term *shemo*. *Shemo* literally means "in his name" but is found to be used when referring to the Biblical story of Jacob wrestling an angel. It was after the combat between Jacob and the angel, for which Jacob was victorious, that Jacob was granted great blessings for his extended family and all of their descendants, and the moment that the defeated angel declared that he would hence be named Israel (Genesis 22). Therefore, it was "in his name" (that of Israel) that the blessings from God for his people were earned.

Even the words shouted out by the *sumo* referee while the combatants are wrestling give a clue. The words belted out are "hake yoi," which in Japanese have absolutely no meaning. However, when those same sounds are translated in the equivalent sounds in Hebrew/Aramaic, they mean "if defeated, let them be." Could this be another reference for Jacob's act of struggling with the angel of God on behalf of his people? Could it be possible that *sumo* was originally an ancient Jewish custom of remembering the event of Jacob's covenant with God, that was later transferred to Japan by way of the descendants of the Lost Tribes of Israel? Did that ritual become part of many Shinto ceremonies, or the remnant of Judaism in Japan before its widespread popularity beginning in the Edo period began to transform the practice into the sport it is today?

There is another *sumo*-related ritual that may have even more in common with the supposed struggle between Jacob and an angel as described in Genesis. In the city of Ehime at the Oyamazumi *jinja* there is a more ritualized display of *sumo*, a one-man *sumo* ceremony that is acted out. This reenactment is understood to be between a mortal and a god. The ceremonial combatant is wrestling the spirit for blessings on the land and people if, metaphorically, victorious.

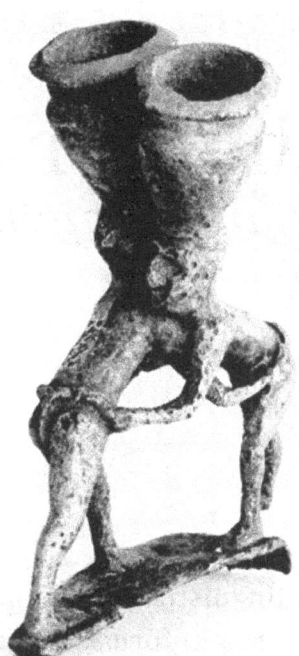

Fig. 39 – An ancient Mesopotamian statuette depicting two men wrestling and dressed remarkably similar to sumo wrestlers.

Chapter 9
Possible Shared Linguistic Roots

C omparative linguistics and etymology, while in some cases straight forward as with studying the connections between Spanish and Portuguese, for example, can be a very tricky and problematic proposition. This is made even more challenging when considering two tongues or scripts that are for most scholars believed to be of very different language family groups, and if it is proposed that those languages may have been one and the same more than twenty-five hundred years ago. It is not a straightforward undertaking. There are layers upon layers of variables that must be considered, like peeling an onion.

This is definitely the case with trying find comparison between ancient Hebrew-Aramaic and Japanese. From the outset, most scholars in these fields of study would not even bother attempting to find common ground between them because of the natural assumptions that there are no connections to be found. Therefore, not only is there little interest in a comparative study of these two languages and systems of writing by mainstream scholars in their modern derivatives, but there is significantly more difficulty getting academics to approach a study of their ancient forms side-by-side. In the case of the Lost Tribes of Israel and early Japanese, some of the considerations one must make are, and not limited to, the following:

1) What was the form of Semitic language spoken and written by the Israelites at the time of the Great Exile?

2) In what ways did the Exile and the relocation thereof impact the spoken and written language?

3) In what ways did the language of the Lost Tribes of Israel evolve as those peoples migrated eastward across Asia?

4) If the Lost Tribes did in fact migrate into Japan, what was the spoken or written form of that language at that moment in history?

5) How have both Hebrew and Japanese changed or evolved from those ancient forms into those represented today?

6) Can one even initially begin to attempt to study these two languages side-by-side, or should there first be an extensive study of early or proto-Hebrew with the languages of the places and people along the proposed migration pattern as outlined in Chapter 1?

Language has always been a prime source or key component of the self-identification for nearly all groups, sub-groups, ethnicities, races, religions, and/or nationalities of mankind from at least the beginnings of recorded history. Every community, large or small, shows great pride in its language, as it should; and every language contains traces in its vocabulary of its linkages with not only former generations but with other linguistic groups with which there was contact. On paper the task seems relatively daunting, which, again, is perhaps why it has not yet been fully attempted in the case of Hebrew/Aramaic and Japanese. It should be noted that there are a couple of comparative linguistic studies undertaken to understand if Japanese and Babylonian/Assyrian are related. The evidence suggests there may be, and, therefore, should raise the question if other Semitic tongues and writing systems related to Babylonian/Assyrian may not also be related. There are significant hurdles, nonetheless. This topic has the potential to be one of the most fascinating areas by which one can discover the possible connections between the ancient Canaanites and early inhabitants of the islands of Japan and must be included in any overall assessment of this potentiality. The work that has been conducted in this area draws up some interesting possibilities that are worth exploring.

Spoken Japanese – Common Etymology

When dissected, there are a number of spoken words in ancient Japanese that are remarkably similar, if not, in some cases, the exact same as spoken words of early Aramaic-Hebrew. Researchers have identified well over five hundred words between these two languages that closely resemble each other, either with pronunciations or meanings. These researchers state that there are many languages, which, if compared together, would seem to share a dozen or so words at best. Several hundred words between two languages is a statistical anomaly, however, and, therefore, cannot be defined as mere coincidence. They say that such an overwhelming number of incidents require it to be considered that some common linguistic background was shared.

Japanese	Hebrew-Aramaic
agatanushi The title given to area leaders given by Emperor Jinmu.	*nasiagudah* group leader
mikado Part of the honorific title given to the emperor.	*migadol* noble
sumera mikoto Another honorific title given to Japanese emperors.	shomron malhuto King of Sumeria
negi Ancient title of Shinto priests.	*nagid* leader
Ashihara The ancient name the Japanese people gave for their country. It means "land of reeds."	*Qanahnah* The ancient name of the Hebrews, Canaan. It means "land of reeds."
Asuka The ancient name of the area of Nara, the location of one of the earliest imperial palaces.	*Hasukkah* at or the tabernacle
misasagi Term for the tomb of a member of the royal family.	*mut sagar* to close the dead

anata/anta you	*Atah/anta* You
hakaru to measure	*haqar* to measure/investigate
horobu to dwindle away or perish	horeb to perish or become ruined
teru to shine	*teurah* illumination
megaru to circle	*magaru* to turn
toru to take	*tol* to take
kamau to care about	*kamal* to sympathize
damaru to become silent	*damam* to become silent
hashiru to hurry or run	*hush* to hurry
nemuru to sleep	*Num* Sleep
kata shoulder	*qatheph* shoulder
tsurai pain	*tzarah* trouble/misfortune
kooru/koori to freeze/ice	*qor* cold
samurau to serve or guard	*shamar* to guard
Samurai Title of the Japanese knightly class/nobility.	*shamarai* profession of guarding
hazukashime disgrace/humiliation	*hadak hashem* disgrace/humiliation
Yamato The ancient name of the Asiatic Japanese people.	*Yehoamato* people of God

Kahana Shinto priest	*koyane/cohen* Upper God and later priest
yashiro dwelling place of God	*yashore* God dwells
kado sacred person	*kadosh* sacred person
sabato ?	*shabbath* sabbath
hazukashima insult	*hazekhashem* insult

Joseph Eidelberg, in his work *The Biblical Hebrew Origin of the Japanese People*, provides approximately five hundred examples of such similar words. Perhaps equally as important as the qualitative linguistic connections are the rare quantitative probabilities of such a set of correlations. Eidelberg states that mathematically there is a one in a million chance that two languages could accidentally share one two-syllable word that has the same rough pronunciation and spelling. There is a one in a hundred million chance of that word having roughly the same meaning. For a shared word with three syllables to share sounds and meanings there is a one in a trillion chance of an accidental correlation. The chance that two languages accidentally share hundreds of similarly sounding words, including spellings and meaning, is astronomical. Therefore, there must be a non-accidental explanation for why Japanese and Hebrew/Aramaic share so many connections. If the theory behind Occam's Razor is to be trusted, the simplest answer is the best answer.

Written Language – Signs of a Shared Alphabet

At first glance, and perhaps even as a secondary or tertiary look, one may get the impression that the Hebrew alphabet, and proto-Hebrew alphabet before it, are in absolutely no way related to written Japanese. It certainly takes one to make a bit of a leap of faith to begin considering the possibility of the correlations and recognize that after thousands of years of evolution and syncretization, two languages that once had a common ancestry may be appear completely different today.

The best way to properly begin identifying possible correlations between Hebrew/Aramaic and Japanese is with an ancient Japanese origin myth. According to the Japanese myths surrounding the origins of all things, the Sun Goddess Amaterasu at one point hid herself in a cave after being frightened by the actions of her brother Susano. As a result, the world went dark. The lower gods begged the upper gods, the *koyane*, to find a way to encourage Amaterasu to some out of her cave hiding place. In addition to several rituals, the *koyane* recited numerous times a holy prayer: *Hifumiyoitsumunanayakokonotowo*. It was this sacred prayer that convinced Amaterasu to emerge from the cave, releasing light once again into the world. This liturgical phrase is such a strong part of Japanese heritage that it was used as the basis for counting: Hi(totsu)-Fu(tatsu)-Mi(tsu)-Yo(tsu)-Mu(tsu)-Nana(tsu)-Ya(tsu)-Kokono(tsu)-Towo. According to Joseph Eidelberg, if one reads this prayer after inserting the appropriate Hebrew vocables, the prayer becomes "Haiafa, mi yotsia; ma na'ne ykakhena tavo," which means "The beautiful, who will bring her out; what should we call out; to entice her to come." Perhaps the early Japanese people, in an effort to immortalize the prayer for future generations, used the prayer as the basis for counting, something repeated thousands of times in one's life.

According to Japanese mythology, a scribe named Wani Kishi introduced *katakana*, a syllabic alphabet, to the people on the islands of Japan. When one looks at the early version of Hebrew, and other such alphabets such as Phoenician, one finds that there are unmistakable similarities with that of the Japanese *katakana* alphabet (now only used by the Japanese for foreign words) and even the *hiragana* alphabet (paired with Chinese ideographs to form native Japanese words). Perhaps this can be explained because in both cultures, the priests in ancient times were traditionally the only literate group and believed that the written language had mystical qualities to it, something that has prevailed in kabbalistic studies to this day. It is theorized by some that Shinto priests, fearing the loss of the sacred alphabet they kept alive to the introduction of Chinese ideographs, proposed hybridizing Japanese to include both Chinese characters and the syllabic alphabets, and thus keeping the remnants of the Hebrew alphabet alive. Nevertheless, there is no evidence to suggest why there is such a strong correlation other than a shared heritage.

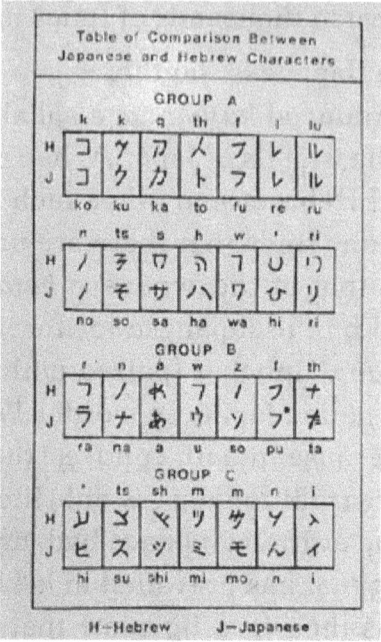

Fig. 40

Alternative Interpretations of Names and Place-names

The names of things and place names of locations can be, and often are, some of the most significant legacies of any culture. This is the case because names are not just words, but carry with them meaning, and with that meaning, a heritage, a history, and an identity. Therefore, cultures all around the world are very sensitive about the names and place names that are used. This is, of course, why many indigenous groups are pushing so hard to have the official place names for their ancestral lands restored from the colonially imposed names. Japan, and the names and place names in Japan, are no exception. Great reverence, for example, has been given to the very name of the country itself, Nihon, which Japanese understand to mean "Land of the Rising Sun." What if, however, the understanding of the meaning of this, and other names, were incorrect?

The Chinese characters used to represent the nation of Japan are 日本, or Nihon, in Romanized Japanese. Again, the contemporary understanding of the meaning of Nihon is either "Land of the Sun," or more fully, "Land of the Rising Sun." These very same characters were read very differently in the early Japanese histories of the *Nihon Shoki*. The proper reading in those early records is that of "Yamato." In ancient Hebrew-Aramaic the name Ya-umato means "Nation of God." An alternative literal reading of the characters for Nihon is "Land of the Book." Could it be that when Chinese script was adopted by the Japanese beginning around the third and fourth centuries CE, a pair of characters were purposely chosen to reflect and maintain the connection with a Jewish heritage, a connection lost over time?

Additionally, the most sacred portion of the central building of a Shinto *jinja*, the *honden*, is written as 本殿 in Chinese characters. According to the contemporary translation of these characters it means "main hall." However, this too may be an incorrect understanding of the original meaning. These very same characters combined can also have the meaning of "Hall of the Book," or literally "Book Hall." While the *honden* does not contain a book or books, the most sacred building of the Jewish Tabernacle and later Solomon's Temple supposedly did. It is believed it housed the Book of the Covenant. Is it plausible that the term *honden*, and a meaning of "Hall of Books," is a remnant of a time when one of the ancient peoples that first migrated to Japan, some of the Lost Tribes of Israel, still associated this sacred building with protecting the Book of the Covenant, even though that holy object was no longer in their possession?

Challenges with Translations and Interpretations

It should be mentioned again that one of the biggest challenges that arises most often with Biblical studies, and most often with using the *Old Testament* as a para-historical document, has been, and still is, the translation and interpretation of these texts. These tales were the first oral traditions passed from generation to generation for hundreds of years before ever being committed to papyrus. There are no original surviving manuscripts of the original transcribed books of the *Torah*, only translations. Even those translations are not the original translations, but copies of much later efforts of preservation. Therefore, there are inconceivably numerable layers to the inaccuracies and changes that have been made to the original histories.

This is the very same set of circumstances that affect the tales the Japanese preserve of their supposed early histories in the *Nihon Shoki* and *Kojiki*. In the case of these documents, the ancient history of the early migrants to the Japanese islands, destroyed in a fire, and only poorly remembered at best, were not even written in a script native to the Japanese, or any peoples such as the Ainu. Instead, they were written in Chinese ideographs largely based on simple phonetic similarities and not equivalent meanings. This means that much of the true meanings of the origin stories associated with ancient Japan may be of little value at all. Satow and Florenz, in *Ancient Japanese Rituals*, explain this best:

[P]eculiarities [exist] in the use of certain

Chinese characters to represent certain Japanese words, from which no trustworthy inferences can be drawn, since the scribes of that age were addicted to numerous irregularities in the use of Chinese ideographs. It is more likely that the [norito], as we have received them, had been transmitted orally, without any material alteration, for generations before they came to be written down. A principle reason for holding this opinion is that they contain not a few words, the meaning of which had been so far forgotten, that no Chinese equivalents could then be found for them; and instead of being translated into Chinese characters, they were written down phonetically. Of these words some have been ingeniously interpreted by modern native philologists, but there remain a good number that have hitherto defied analysis, and the preservation of such unintelligible words, instead of substituting something that could be readily understood, is a powerful argument I favour of the antiquity of the present text of those *norito* in which they occur.

While it is certainly possible to get a general notion from these ancient documents no matter how butchered they may be now, it is entirely possible that a vast majority of the truth will be lost forever. Is it possible that the original histories of the ancient Israelites and Japanese, if somehow available, would reveal the details of a shared heritage, the knowledge of which has been lost over time?

Hermeneutical Distance and Pre-judgement

The influence and impact that Chinese script had, not just the immediate effect it had on the way by which Japanese was written, and with the transformation of some of the pronunciation of Japanese in order to fit it, was more profound in other ways. Chinese script did not find its way to Japan independently but was a part of a much greater change that was taking place on the islands as a result of closer geo-political relations with the mainland and imperial China, and alongside the spread of both Buddhism and Confucianism.

This spoken and written linguistic transformation was not confined only to the Yayoi-Yamato transitional period. The adoption of a hybridized written language was cumbersome, and it could be argued that the incongruencies and inefficiencies were never really fully flushed out until the Meiji period, morphing further as a result of the introduction of foreign "words, concepts, idioms, and symbols."

> In that kind of climate, there were not enough people who were reflective and critical, not only about the differences between Western and Japanese languages, but also, and more important, about the different conventions employed by Westerners and the Japanese in their perceptions of the textures of human experience".

This description could be applied to the initial adoption of Chinese script. For example, some adopted the Chinese script based on their relative equivalence to meanings of Japanese words, while others simply swapped or borrowed Chinese pictographs for Japanese words on the basis that they had similar sounds, irrespective of the actual meaning behind the Chinese script.

All of this proved to change the social, political, and cultural landscape of Japan, one that would evolve from the fourth to sixth centuries CE into something almost unrecognizable two centuries later. One area in which this change with Japanese manifested itself was in the re-recorded histories of ancient Japan, the *Nihon Shoki* and *Kojiki.* As already mentioned, the conflicts that raged from roughly the sixth and eighth centuries CE between the collective supporters of the adoption of Buddhism as the state religion over those that claimed to defend the preservation of Shintoism as the nativist faith led to virtual civil war. One of the byproducts of that conflict was the destruction of an entire cache of sacred and historical documents – the entirety of Japan's recorded heritage up to that point. When the dust finally settled, and something of a balance was reached politically, and, therefore, somewhat religiously, an attempt was made to preserve what could of the remaining records and remembrances of Japanese ancient history. Hence the *Nihon Shoki* and *Kojiki.*

There is no denying that the completely new political and religious reality of Japan in the beginning of the eighth century CE, when these new records were produced, influenced the wording, language, interpretations, meanings, and emphases in those re-recorded epochs. While it cannot be concluded with any assurance that there were explicit intentions of those tasked with writing, and those commissioning the new records, to establish a wholly new narrative of Japan from the ancient

145

period up to the Taika era, it stands to reason that there were at least unintentional outcomes to that effect. The geo-political upheaval of the Meiji period, including the chasm that developed between a traditional and modernizing Japan, is another example of how history affects linguistics.

> This intriguing political development had direct bearing on the linguistic and thought forms that are problematic for us now.

Hebrew/Aramaic, too, it must be mentioned, underwent significant metamorphoses. Just as there were points of great transformation in Japan's history that at least partially affected the language, spoken and written, the People of the Covenant faced similar moments; the period spent in Egypt, the Exodus, gradual, yet temporary, unification during the imperial era, and the Exiles, just to mention a few. For an additional presentation of linguistic connections, especially between Hebrew-Aramaic and Japanese place names and names of people, see Prof. Shachan's work.

Chapter 10
Comparison Between the Japanese Emperor and the Jewish "Priestly King"

A s already stated, the monarchies of both the Kingdom of Israel and Imperial Japan have traditions of considering their monarchs to be "priestly kings," or rulers that are not just divinely appointed or ordained as the supreme authority of the land, as is the case with nearly all monarchies, but have a special calling to look after the spiritual wellbeing of their people and to serve as one of many holy messengers. There are several characteristics of this idea of "priestly kingship" that both cultures share in common. Beginning with the first king of Israel, Saul, the king of Israel was, due to his special nature as a representative of heaven on earth, a participant in the religious affairs of the Israelites, just as the emperors of Japan played active roles in some of the most important Shinto ceremonies.

Emperor Jinmu

Even before Jinmu Tennou came to power, the name of the assumed first emperor of Japan according to the ancient records (*shiki*), Japan already had an existing legacy of imperial lineage. How, therefore, is Emperor Jinmu connected to that lineage? It is estimated by scholars that Emperor Jinmu began his reign, after conquering the islands of Japan, around 300 CE. Several scholars have argued that Jinmu was the leader of a group of the Lost Ten Tribes, and that after arriving in Japan, his group began conquering the indigenous peoples already on the islands, such as the Ainu. McLeod, for example, and without any basis for the claim, states that he and his people were able to do this because of the superiority of their Jewish heritage over the inferior aboriginal peoples of the islands. As will be described in much greater detail later, there is room to suggest a very different narrative (see Chapter 11).

The available evidence, nonetheless, describes a group of more racially Asiatic people, under the direction of someone, at least according to mythology, known as Jinmu Tennou, arriving in the islands of Japan in and around 300 CE, first on the island of Kyushu. This group did not bring with them what would later be the Shinto faith. It is much more likely that the early remnants of Shintoism were already part of the indigenous cultures of at least the Ainu, as, the author will claim later, they were the possible the descendants of the Lost Tribes of Israel (see Chapter 11). The exact origins of this migrant group that crossed from Korea are unknown. However, it is entirely possible that, as will be further explored, they may have been another wave of descendants of the Lost Tribes of Israel. The author argues that this wave of migrants was the remnants of the second exile of what remained of the Kingdom of Judah, and the tribes of Judah and Benjamin (see Chapter 11). The group led by Jinmu may have certainly begun to dominate the islands, as mentioned in the collective mythologies, but they did so at the expense of the earlier immigrant Israelites.

Egami Namio, in the middle of the twentieth century, was one of the first to suggest that the myth of Emperor Jinmu was the story of the Korean, Asiatic peoples that migrated into Japan, only to eventually dominate the islands with its culture, language (Chinese), religion (Buddhism), and political structure. First settling on the island of Kyushu, Namio states that these Korean tribes gradually subdued the true Yamato peoples of the islands of Honshu and Shikoku. Therefore, the animosity described of Jinmu and his people toward the Ainu, for example, may have very well been left over from the very same geo-political divisiveness that existed in the Holy Land prior to the First Exile. In order to establish legitimacy, and therefore help make subjugation under his regime more palatable, it is likely that Emperor Jinmu plugged himself into an existing imperial narrative along with assimilating his people's religious traditions into the existing framework. Isaiah Ben-Dosan best summarized this by stating the "myth, legend, and history" promoted by the conquering regime was formulated in a way "as to flatter the reigning dynasty." It certainly would not be the first time a conquering group has followed a similar formula of conquest (Chinggis Khan in China). For anyone familiar with the traditional racial bias of the Japanese, Namio's suggestion is remarkable. Did a second wave of Israelites in exile follow their brethren eastward across Asia? Did that group linger in the area of Eastern China and Korea long enough to assimilate into the cultures of that region? Did those very same people subsequently carry with them an entirely morphed set of beliefs and practices when migrating to the islands of Japan?

The Japanese have tried to maintain, perhaps not explicitly so, that their race is somehow unique to Asia, almost a racial island on the physical islands they inhabit. It is almost as if they have collective amnesia about the true nature of their ethnic and racial origins. This general perspective may be the basis for the racial superiority promoted from the time of Jinmu up to and during the Meiji Period to help justify Japan's regional imperialism. To this day there is an underlying sense among the Japanese that the Korean, Chinese, and other Asiatic peoples are inferior, to the point that even descendants of Korean migrants born in Japan are kept at a distance socially.

Official Imperial Title

Some scholars mention the official imperial title assumed by all emperors of Japan, as stated in the *Kojiki* or *Nihon Shoki* ancient texts about Japan's early history, as evidence that Emperor Jinmu was carrying on a legacy that stretched back from before his time onward. The title of the emperor was *kamu yamato iwarebiko sumera mikoto*. According to a few, this is a title that predates Japanese, thus predating Emperor Jinmu, and is the Japanese form of an early Hebrew title that means, when the sounds are converted into Hebrew-Aramaic, "His Imperial Majesty of Samaria, the Exalted founder of the Hebrew Nation of Yahweh."

Imperial Symbolism

The imperial crest of the Japanese monarchy is that of a chrysanthemum, or for some, a sunflower-shaped flower, and has been the symbol of the royal house from ancient times. This same imagery was common among the ancient Assyrians in the carved relief tablets depicting the tales of their deities. The symbol would also appear in Israel after the Persians allowed the people to return to their homeland. The Second Temple, commissioned by King Herod, had decorative stones included with this same crest of the chrysanthemum or sunflower. Did this symbology find its way into Judaism by way of the exiles in Persia, as well as follow some of those descendants with them to Japan?

Fig. 41 – chrysanthemum-like crest above Herod's gate

Fig. 42 – chrysanthemum-like crest on a clay tablet of ancient Assyria

One of the most iconic of all royal symbols from the Kingdom of Israel is the star or shield of David, the symbol used to represent not just the secular nation of Israel, but Judaism as well. The same imagery, called a *kagome*, has been incorporated in the construction of Shinto *jinja* from ancient times, as found on every lamp leading up to the original Ise shrine in Kiyoto, for example.

Fig. 43 – one of several lanterns at the entrance to Ise jinja in Kiyoto

Other such examples of the Star-of-David-like crests are the *asa no ha*, used by the Komiya and Magaribuchi clans, as well as the municipal regalia from such cities as Nishi no miya, Oumuta, Otaru, Wakkanai, and Fukuchiyama. Could this represent a connection between the royal lineage of the clans of Japan with the Kingdom of Israel?

Fig. 44 – asa no ha

Fig. 45 – Nishinomiya city crest

Fig. 46 – Oumuta city crest

Fig. 47 – Wakkanai city crest

Fig. 48 – Fukuchiyama city crest

Menorah Symbology

Similar to the Star of David symbology being found at numerous sites and in the crests of Japanese municipalities and family/clan iconography, the image of the *menorah* has also been found in several places. In one such case, a *menorah*-like emblem was identified at the threshold of the holiest part of the Yamato Okunitama *jinja* near Mima city in Tokushima Prefecture on the island of Shikoku. When asked in an NHK television program on the subject why such a symbol might be part of such a holy Shinto structure, one of the head priests of the shrine mentioned that the Tokushima area was a stronghold of the Hata clan (please see Chapter 11 for further information about the Hata clan's connection to the overall subject). The Hata clan is believed to be the dominant clan of Israelites that migrated at some point to Japan around the third or fourth century CE. "Yamato Okunitama," the name of the shrine, could be translated in Japanese as "The Great Nation of Yamato." And, if "Yamato" is, as previously stated, correctly understood to mean "people of Yahweh," then the name of the shrine is "The Great Nation of the People of Yahweh."

At the site of another Shinto shrine in Tokushima Prefecture, Shinmei *jinja*, an image identical to the one at Yamato Okunitama *jinja* was found in the stonework of ruins of part of that shrine's property. The supposed descendants of those that originally built this very ancient shrine, now mostly in ruins, were tracked down by the very same NHK television production team. One of those interviewed on the subject reported that his ancestors passed down numerous protocols related to observances at the shrine. One such observance was that a fire at the shrine must remain lit at all times, very similar to a tradition at the Jewish Tabernacle, and later at the First and Second temples, that lamps must remain burning at all times (Exodus 27:20). It was also stated that about halfway up Mt. Tsurugi in the very same prefecture, and referenced in an ancient local document called Awashi, there is a cave in which the Israelites deposited a great "treasure." Unfortunately, when the NHK production team visited the cave, it was observed that the interior of the cave was completely blocked by massive boulders. There is, of course, a great deal of speculation as to whether the Jewish descendants of the Lost Tribes of Israel had in fact left something inside the cave, and what it could be. Everything from portions of Solomon's treasures to the Ark of the Covenant has been rumored.

Imperial Holy Objects

According to the mythology of early Japan, three objects possessing incredible power were passed on from emperor to emperor from ancient times and are believed to still be held in the imperial palace to this day, only visible to the emperor. These three objects are a mirror-like object called *yata no kagami*, a large crystal bead or ball called *yasaka no magatama*, and a sword called *kusanagi no tsurugi*. Dr. Chikao Fujisawa of Kyushu Imperial University believes that the three sacred objects of King Solomon – Solomon's Table, Shamir, and Solomon's Seal – share similar forms. Solomon's Table was supposedly a special table made of wood and mirror top, which gave King Solomon the ability of remote viewing, among other powers. The Shamir was, according to the Jewish mythology of King Solomon, a device that allowed for cutting hard objects such as diamonds. Could this be the "sword" of Imperial Japan's sacred objects? Solomon's Seal was believed to be a ring-like object with four magical stones encrusted in it that gave Solomon the ability to control the four elements: earth, air, fire and water. Could the "bead" of Imperial Japan's holy trinkets be one of the remaining precious stones from Solomon's Seal?

Cities of Peace

Ben Ami Shillony points out that even the meanings of the names of the imperial cities of these two cultures are similar. Jerusalem is now associated as the city that was the great historical capital of the ancient Jews as well as the modern state of Israel. However, it was not always so. King David moved the capital in around 1000 BCE from Hebron, and built a new capital he named Yerushalayim, Jerusalem, or City of Peace. On the other side of the planet, the Empress Gemmei, in approximately 710 CE, moved the Japanese capital to the area of modern-day Nara, and called it Heijokyou, or Citadel of Peace. About eighty years later the capital was moved to what is now Kiyoto, and that new capital was named Heiankyou, or City of

Peace. Kiyoto to this day is considered by the Japanese people to be the place of spiritual and cultural birth, just as Jerusalem is to the Jews.

Chapter 11
The Ainu Question

T he Ainu people are one of the original or indigenous peoples of the islands of Japan. Racially speaking, they are clearly and distinctively not mongo-
loid, with fair skin, reddish-brown hair, round eyes, and
broad noses. There has been a great deal of speculation
as to their origins for hundreds of years with numerous
theories postulated. Unfortunately, nearly all of the preservation of Ainu traditions was passed on orally until
roughly the Meiji era. During the Meiji period, the Japanese government embarked on a sort of purification
quest across the islands, actively eradicating anything
culturally, religiously, racially, linguistically, or otherwise
that was not part of the growing ideals of Japanese nationalism. Regrettably, much of the Ainu cultural and linguistic heritage was lost in the process. The Ainu tale of the
"Song That Was Sung and Danced by Oynakamuy and His
Wife" shares an experience of a Japanese feudal lord that
sends a group of men for the purpose of taking a married
woman by force or payment to the husband as his bride.
The story describes one of those policies, i.e., mixing the

"racial impurities" out of the Ainu.

Much of the supposedly early research into the past of the Ainu was less about trying to genuinely solve the mystery of their origins, and more about justifying the imperial policies of the Meiji. This included research by Western writers. Nicholas McLeod, the Scotch missionary, tried to claim that the Ainu were an inferior indigenous race compared to the more physically robust specimen of Asiatic people that came later to the islands. He even stated, incorrectly, that the term *ainu* was the Japanese term for the people meaning "despicable dogs," and that the name *ainu* did not exist in their language. We know clearly now that *ainu*, along with *utari*, is one of the terms the people use for themselves and was not a derogatory term given to them by the Japanese.

In fact, the name the Ainu have for Japan is *Samoro*. One of their terms for their people is *Samai*. Could these terms be in some way related to the Japanese word for *samurai*, "one who serves?" There is an old mythological story that tells how the ancestors of the *samurai* came from the west and traveled across Asia, before ending up in Japan in the six hundreds BCE, and that they were the priestly class of their people. Perhaps the *samurai* were descended from the priesthood, or "those that serve God," of the Lost Tribes of Israel that found their way to Japan, and the Japanese name that came to be used for this elite social group is a derivative of *samai*. Even the term in the Ainu language for gods, *kamui*, is very close to the Japanese word for the gods/spirits, *kami*.

It has not been until more recently that fair scholarly research has been done on these people, uncovering more about their true nature. Due to the scholarly bias toward the more Asiatic Japanese, at the expense of any other indigenous peoples of the islands such as the Ryukyus, any connections the Ainu may have with the links with the Lost Tribes of Israel and Judaism have been largely overlooked. Whereas McLeod argued that the descendants of the Lost Tribes of Israel arrived in and subjugated the islands of Japan after the Ainu had arrived, some of the latest research on this subject is revealing a very different, and quite remarkable alternative narrative.

Genetic Studies

The latest gene and DNA studies of the Ainu have uncovered that the Ainu are almost exclusively of haplogroup D, with only small traces of other haplogroups. They also carry the rare YAP gene sequence. This means that the Ainu were able to maintain a relative homogeneity, despite the close proximity to subsequent migrations of Asiatic peoples onto the islands. As reported previously, haplogroup D and YAP sequence have their origins in Southwest Asia. The connection between the Ainu and Southwest Asia was further developed through a series of DNA studies that ultimately identified genetic links between them and an early ethnicity from the Upper Nile called the Annu (similar to Ainu?), and with the Micmaq Ainu of Eastern Canada.

Fig. 49

The map of Fig. 49 shows the accepted migration pattern of haplogroup D from the Nile River initially to Southwest Asia, then on into Central and South Asia, before passing eastward to East Asia and Japan. These people may have taken on the name of their primary deity, Anu, Egyptian Atun, Akkadian Anu, or El among the early Canaanite (later Yahweh among the Israelites). Based on the early patterns of migration, and the fact that the spiritual world of the peoples of North Africa and Southwest Asia were intimately connected and syncretized, this is perhaps another possibility or version of the narrative that has not yet been proposed or suggested by other researchers of the connection between the Lost Tribe of Israel with Japan, and by extension with Shintoism – one first postulated by Alice Linsley in her blog post in 2014 titled "Solving the Ainu Mystery."

Ainu Origins

It is entirely plausible that the origins of the Ainu began with a people along the Nile River near the holy city of Heliopolis (City of the Sun, originally called Annu by the aboriginal peoples for which it was a religious sanctuary), the principal site of the worship of Atun (Aten) and the monotheistic worship thereof. The cult of Atun was first introduced by Akhenaten during his reign around the middle thirteen hundreds BCE, with the sun portrayed in iconography with the Atun. According to what Egyptologists have been able to discover, this new faith was not well received by the traditional priestly class specifically, and the populace in general. This may be due to the systematic persecution under Akhenaten of the other Egyptian deities and their respective cults, especially the primary state deity, Amun. One of the ways in which Akhenaten and the priests of this new tradition tried to make the cult more palatable was to draw connections between the cult of sun worship of the god Ra and Atun. Thus, Heliopolis became, for a time, associated with the worship of the combined nature of Aten and Ra, as Atun-ra. There is an Egyptian inscription that reads "Temples of the God Seth of the Cities of the Annu people's Tera-neter (priest of God)."

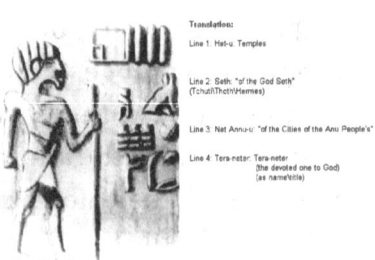

Translation:
Line 1: Het-u: Temples

Line 2: Seth: "of the God Seth" (Tchut\Thoth\Hermes)

Line 3: Net Annu-u: "of the Cities of the Anu People's"

Line 4: Tera-neter: Tera-neter (the devoted one to God) (as name/title)

Fig. 50

If the *Old Testament*, and the timeline accepted by most Egyptologists and *Old Testament* scholars, are to be believed, the people that later become referred to as the Israelites, the descendants of Israel, were a subjugated people living in Egypt, and had been for a couple of hundred years by count, at the time the cult of Atun was popularized. It would not be a stretch to assume that other Egyptian cults, along with that of Atun, played a significant role in shaping and influencing the beliefs of those captive Israelites. This may be most recognized by the direct relationship between the iconographic image of the apis bull with the sun disc between its horns from the worship of Hathor and the brazen bull created and worshiped after the Exodus by the Israelites according to the *Old Testament*. The Israelites blended bits and pieces of Egyptian cults with their own inherited beliefs.

Fig. 51 – Egyptian depiction of the apis bull as Ra

Fig. 52 – illustration of the golden idol of a calf supposedly created by the Israelites during the Exodus

Akhenaten died roughly around 1336 BCE, and the Exodus is dated to around 1270 BCE, and an approximately sixty-year period during which there was a backlash against the cult of Atun and restoration of the traditional pantheon of polytheistic gods. This is where the story of Moses comes in. Moses, it should be argued, who may have been of mixed Canaanite and Egyptian blood based on the Biblical story, supposedly converted from the traditional Egyptian religious system to one that resembled the monotheistic cult of Atun. The claim can further be made that, believing to be acting on behalf of Atun, or known to the Israelites as El, Moses campaigned to get those people released from slavery. Following this line of reasoning, it was Moses, Aaron, Jacob, and the other converts to, or perhaps, practitioners and priests that led the "faithful" of Atun (El), that led the early Israelites to migrate away from Egypt into the Levant, settling among the various tribal groups there.

Nearly all of those groups among whom the Israelites were conquering and settling, including many of the Israelites themselves, had their own proprietary deities, some of which may have been based on or influenced by the Egyptian polytheistic traditions led by Amun-ra, with which the God of Moses was in constant competition. There is an interesting note made by Satow and Florenz in *Japanese Sacred Rituals*.

> [T]he priests of the temples to which offerings were sent by the Mikado entered in succession, and took the places severally assigned to them. The horses which formed a part of the offerings were next brought in from the Mikado's stable, and all the congregation drew near, while the reader recited or read the *norito*. This reader was a member of the priestly family or

tribe of Nakatomi, who traced their descent back to Amenokoyane, one of the principal advisers attached to the sun-goddess' grandchild when he first descended on earth.

The name "Amenokoyane" literally means "The Priest of Amen" in both early Japanese and Hebrew-Aramaic. Are the Ainu, and consequently Shintoism, descended from Israelites that still maintained aspects of Egyptian spiritualism and cult practices as part of a greater amalgamation of traditions held by the early Jews as a whole?

It is from this point forward that the narrative already outlined about the migration of the Israelites later from the Holy Land eastward, leaving their mark along the way, picks up. It could further be suggested, therefore, that the mythology supported by some as the story behind how the Jews and Judaism arrived in Japan, that of the tale of Emperor Jinmu leading some of the Lost Tribesmen across Asia to the islands and conquering it, is not entirely correct, at least not entirely so, and that it was the Ainu people, the people of Annu, perhaps the descendants of the Lost Tribes of Israel from the First Exile, who brought those traditions with them well before a later wave of Asiatic migrants arrived. It was this later wave of more Asiatic migrants, and, it is argued by this author that they were a subsequent wave of Israelite exiles from perhaps the Second Exile, that brought an affinity for Chinese culture (linguistics), spirituality (Buddhism), and imperial governing philosophy (Confucianism) that, beginning around the third or fourth century CE, would lead to a renewed gradual clash between these two different worlds (think Kingdom of Judah and Kingdom of Samaria).

Prof. Avigdor Shachan made a very interesting claim in his book, *In the Footsteps of the Lost Ten Tribes*, that could arguably shed light on another possible understanding of this chapter of the story. His thorough evaluation of the *Kojiki* and *Nihon Shoki* reveals that there were actually two groups of post-Exilic Jews making their way across Asia, splitting at about the Central Asian part of the journey, one heading West-Northwest to the Korean Peninsula and the other south into India before finally arriving in Korea. The reason he derives from the texts for this split was due to a disagreement over which tribe should lead the expedition. The two rivals, the tribes of Ephraim and Manasseh, could no longer set aside their quarrels, and parted ways. According to Prof. Shachan, the first wave of Israelites, led by Manasseh, did not pause long before crossing the strait to settle in the Japanese islands. The other wave, led by Ephraim, and containing the largest body of the Israelite elite, lingered in China and Korea for several hundred years it seems, and only made the final leap across to the islands in order to flee the political persecution imposed upon them by a growing threat from a series of increasingly imperialistic Chinese regimes. This group of lingering descendants of Jews would have absorbed not just the cultural, linguistic, and religious norms of the land in which they settled, dominated by the Chinese, Buddhism, and Confucianism, but racial mixing would have been difficult to avoid. In light of these conclusions, the origins of the clash between the Ainu and the later wave of migrants becomes clear, as well as the characteristics thereof.

It could be additionally proclaimed, again, as does Alice Linsley, that based on the information regarding the genetics of the Ainu versus the Japanese people, the data points more toward the explanation that the Japanese people have the haplogroup D with the YAP gene sequence because that people inherited it from both their Ainu and mixed migrant ancestors. Even before the Meiji period, but with increased zeal during that era, as previously mentioned, the government tried, among other policies, to "purify" the race by forcing the women to intermarry with the more Asiatic Japanese. Therefore, the only original carriers of the leftover D haplogroup along with the YAP sequence from the Middle East were the Ainu. The Ainu people of Japan are descended from the Annu aboriginal people of the Upper Nile, the first rulers of Lower Egypt. And, if we are to believe Prof. Shachan's additional theory, the genetic questions are also made much clearer.

Do the Japanese refer to their nation then as "the land of the rising sun" because of its known place in the Far East, the connection the sun has with their ancestral faith, and the relationship of the sun rising on the east of the tabernacle/temple? Entirely possible. Did these same migrants later find their way into North America and settle in Northeast Canada? Entirely possible. It should also be mentioned, at least in brief, that there are numerous other coincidental linkages between the early Israelites and Japanese with other African peoples of the Upper Nile region. What this ultimately means, therefore, is that the story of the relationship between the early Israelites and Judaism with the islands, people, and faith of Japan is really only part of the greater migration narrative from early humans from sub-Saharan Africa into the corners of Eurasia. This does not mean the Ainu are the first people to inhabit the Japanese islands. There is plenty of evidence to suggest that migrants found their way to the islands as early as the last ice age. The Ainu, therefore, may not be the first inhabitants of the Japanese islands at all, but a wave subsequent to others coming out of Siberia. In fact, it is most likely that what we understand to be the Ainu culture was originally more of a blending of the first peoples from after the Paleolithic period with the Israelites. The name that the Yakut people of Siberia give their shamans, aïy-oïuna, is oddly similar to *ainu*. The Ainu, or as proposed, some of the descendants of the Lost Tribes of Israel, experienced some syncretization of their culture, language, and beliefs as they moved eastward from the Levant, and eventually landed in Japan. The added totemic aspects of their spiritual expression were just a more recent part of that blending effect.

Unfortunately, since the Ainu had no written language for the thousands of years of their history, and it was not until the modern era from which attempts began to be made to record the Ainu oral folklore and histories, very little of the original meanings, illusions, or symbolism of these tales can be understood or deciphered. The Ainu *yukara*, for example, or folk tales, are full of stories told from the point of view of spirits, or *kami* (animal, plant, solid object, personified gods as heroes, or natural elements deities), but are assumed to be understood symbolically rather than literally.

It does not help matters that many of the preserved myths were first transcribed into Japanese before being translated again into other languages, thus perpetuating potential loss of accuracy. Additionally, much of the heritage of the Ainu language was systematically eradicated entirely. Place names on the islands and terms used for geographic reference are just one example. Romyn Hitchcock, in his study of the Ainu peoples, *The Aino of Yezo, Japan*, mentions the sad fact that when the Japanese adopted Chinese ideograms these symbols were haphazardly applied to place names and geographic terms of reference used for hundreds of years.

> These characters have meanings which may or may not throw light upon the origin of the name. For example, Otaru is an Aino place-name, meaning "sandy road." The reading of the Chinese characters is "small cask." Many examples of this kind show that the meaning of the Chinese characters may be very misleading.

How much of the indigenous language of the islands of Japan, of the Ainu, was completely wiped out, making way for a completely inaccurate interpretation of their myths, beliefs, and collective identity?

Continued Mythologies

Despite commonly being categorized as being a polytheistic people based on their largely animistic spiritual heritage, the Ainu often referred in the oral traditions that began to be written down in the mid to late 1800s to a single all-powerful deity that had dominion over all other spirits and natural concerns. This gives a description of a people with a more mono-lateral understanding of their physical and spiritual reality than has been previously conceded. This, of course, fits with the development of Shintoism. For example, it is believed that the Ainu worshiped the Sun, something consistent

169

with the supposed animistic nature of their belief system. However, alternative interpretations of this suggest that the Ainu did not worship the Sun, but, rather, the force behind the Sun. This deification of the Sun may have led to the Shinto worship of Amaterasu, the goddess (or god) of the Sun. It is perhaps more accurate to say that the spirituality of the Ainu was not animistic, but was much more sophisticated and, therefore, more consistent with a people that had a well-developed system of belief.

According to the creation mythologies of the Ainu, this supreme god named Ainu rak guru, or Aioina by some, is believed to have been the creator of all, including mankind. In fact, the name Ainu rak guru means "a person like man," and it is believed that Aioina created man in his likeness. Aioina, after having first brought order to chaos, and then creating all of the vegetative life of the earth, proceeded to make man from the earth. Their god, they believe, is the Lord of Hosts, and takes an active interest in the affairs of man.

The Ainu understood that their god, while supreme, used intermediaries, or special chiefs, to carry out divine will, not unlike the tradition of prophets among the Jews. These and other such stories are not only found to be the basis of the opening scenes of the Book of Genesis but are also described in the opening of both the *Kojiki* and *Nihon Shoki*, the two accepted histories of ancient Japan. It is entirely plausible that the reason the *Kojiki* and *Nihon Shoki* begin with similar tales is not because they belong to the Asiatic Japanese that came to dominate Japan, but because the tales had long been forged with the identity of the peoples of the islands long before anyone could recall any separate histories between the Ainu and later Asiatic migrations.

Origins of Shintoism

It must also be made clear that the proto-Shinto beliefs brought to Japan by the Ainu are not, and should not, be equated with Judaism, whether proto-Judaism or the more contemporary form. Judaism, in whatever form it took during, and immediately after the Babylonian Exile, while keeping a lot of the characteristics, evolved considerably as the Lost Tribes migrated through the lands of Asia, and continued to evolve even after settling in Japan. Shintoism and Judaism are now two completely distinct religious traditions that may have once shared a common spiritual ancestry, as Buddhism once did with Hinduism. Nevertheless, Shintoism, or the possibly changed form of Judaism, was, and is, unique to and from the origins of the Ainu peoples.

As previously mentioned, Shintoism, as a term referring to the early set of religious practices and beliefs of Japan, was a title first assigned during the Meiji period for the purpose of making a distinction between those traditions, Buddhism, and/or Christianity, the latter of which was gaining a considerable number of converts.

> [T]he Meiji government legally separated Shinto and Buddhism, signifying a sudden undoing by fiat of the historical pattern of a Shinto-Buddhist amalgam (*Shin-Butsu shuugou*). Clearly, the new government wished to depend only on the native Shinto to provide it with "cosmic legitimation."

The spiritual understanding of the Ainu peoplezof the Jewish priestly class and a head dress of sorts worn by

171

the chieftains of the Ainu.

The details of the varying similarities between the priestly garments and accessories between Shinto *shinshoku* and Jewish priests, especially of the earlier epoch of that faith, have already been outlined. One object that shows a strong correlative sign between those faiths is the respective phylactery worn about the forehead. If, as is argued by this author, the Ainu spiritual traditions are the root of Shintoism, and the Ainu are in part descendants of the Lost Tribes of Israel, then the discovery of a phylactery-like object, called a *shaba umpe*, that resembles that worn by Jewish priests and their Shinto counterparts is, therefore, nothing shocking. On the contrary, it could or would be expected. These special headdresses were only worn on special spiritual occasions, as is the case in Judaism and Shintoism. Are these Ainu headdresses the morphed remnants of the *tefillin* of Judaism?

Fig. 54 – Ainu elder wearing the bear headdress

Fig. 55

Lost Identity

It can be concluded that the Ainu, or some of the descendants of the remnants of the Lost Tribes of Israel, were an established culture on the islands of Japan by 300 BCE, corresponding with the end of the Joumon Period and the transition into the Yayoi. Further, a major wave of Asiatic migration took place from the mainland to the islands of Japan around the third or fourth century CE, coinciding roughly with the beginning of the Yamato Period, and began to displace the Ainu as the dominant culture on the islands, beginning with the island of Kyuushuu. According to the ancient Japanese text, the "Shinsen Shoujiroku Koushou," a kind of record of genealogy of the early Japanese, it is stated that this second wave of Israelites, consisting of about 190,000 persons, was led by the Hata clan, and that this group had come out of the steppe somewhere near what is modern day Kazakhstan before settling in Manchuria for a time. As already mentioned, the Asiatic peoples that migrated and colonized Japan adopted much of the Ainu spiritual way of life as well as perhaps twisting their histories for their own nationalistic purposes, in much of the same way that the Nahuatl people in North America, most commonly referred to as the Aztecs, assimilated the cultures of Central Mexico after migrating to and conquering those lands.

Not only did the Yamato Period, with the influx of peoples from the mainland, whether this wave of Asiatic peoples was or was not a later migration of Israelites, usher in a dramatic socio-demographic change to the islands, but those colonizers brought with them their own brand of governance, values, and spiritualism; a set of norms that contrasted with that of the previously dominant peoples of the islands, the Ainu. Whereas the Ainu seemed to have no lingering connections with the mainland, the colonizing Asiatic group's identity was still firmly grounded in the relationship with the cultures that dominated the mainland, namely the Chinese. These people brought with them Buddhism, Confucianism, and a unique and separate nationalism from what they found on the islands. These beliefs, philosophies, and identities clashed with that of the Ainu. This clash of these two worlds led to the systematic displacement by the new colonizers of the Ainu from their lands, their traditions and customs, their livelihood, and, in general, their unique identity as a people. The colonizers appropriated what they wanted and discarded what they did not of the heritage of those they encountered. The clearest example of how this tumultuous transition took place was with the struggle between the survival of Shintoism against the growing dominance of Buddhism.

The Ainu had, by the sixth century CE, been removed geo-politically on most of the islands, to be replaced by a very Confucian and Chinese imperial system of governance brought by the conquerors. Buddhism was inseparable from that system, as well as the nationalism tied closely to it. Despite the adoption by these colonizers of the collective historical heritage of ancient Japan, or at

174

least their own version of it, Shintoism was viewed as a threat to the new imperial regime, and, like the Ainu themselves, needed to be eliminated. Despite all efforts by the early imperial Japanese regimes to wipe out all traces of the Ainu, enough of that people remained, in marginalized communities in remote areas, to pass on some traces of their blood and heritage. Shintoism, with the help of several strong clans between the seventh and eighth centuries, survived, though, more as a syncretic form with Buddhism.

Unfortunately, the eradication of Ainu histories, their early beliefs, customs, and practices have been so thorough since the third and fourth centuries CE that the full picture of their possible relationship with the Ten Lost Tribes of Israel, Judaism, and the Joumon-Yayoi-Yamato periods of transition may never be uncovered. This is tragic, not only for the loss in general of the historical enlightenment this knowledge would and could provide about the ancient world, but, much more importantly, because it may mean the almost complete disappearance of the memory of their collective heritage for the remnants of the Ainu people.

Chapter 12
Room for Further Investigation

While it is clear that there is material from which further exploration and investigation into the correlations between Judaism and Shintoism, and the ancient Israelites cum Lost Tribes of Israel and the Ainu peoples of early Japan, there are even more documents or other evidence that have yet to be studied fully. To date, this topic, as a subject of scholarly study, has not received the attention that it deserves. If there is, as perhaps the evidence suggests, a genuine connection between these seemingly unrelated peoples, religious traditions, and parts of the ancient world, then not only would this be a revelation about the histories of these two cultures, but it would also open up a world of possibly new understandings between the ancient peoples that came and went between Western and Eastern Asia.

Call for Further Scholarship

It is true that the body of existing knowledge and available evidence, both artifacts and textual, is not as extensive as perhaps found with other areas of historical studies. There could potentially be more uncovered if scholars wanted to make a more concerted effort. Unfortunately, and in the assessment of this author, scholars tend to avoid diving into shallow water with limited resources. They prefer larger, more voluminous bodies of water from which they can more easily postulate conclusions. Scholars also tend to shy away from controversies, or controversial topics, and prefer calmer seas. Oftentimes, those that do brave the choppy waters risk the potential of being ridiculed and labeled as nothing more than para-historians.

It should be hoped, however, that more researchers will be encouraged or inspired to take up the challenge of making serious efforts to uncover further truths related to the possible correlation between Judaism and Shintoism, whether those conclusions eventually find more substantial proof of the common heritage of these faiths or disprove the hypothesis altogether.

Esoteric Texts

The textual sources referred to for part of the overall investigation, the *Nihon Shoki*, *Kojiki*, and *Old Testament/Torah*, for example, and despite being the only ancient documents traditionally accepted in the case of this topic as it turns out, are not the only possible written evidence with something to reveal. There are a number of supposed ancient texts that have survived as rewritten versions that scholars and historians have, for a number of reasons, not included as the documents in the body of evidence. Some of these ancient texts include the following:

Sendai Kuji Hongi Taiseikyou (also known as the Kojiki-72)

Hotsuma Tsutaye

The Takenouchi Documents

The Chronicles of Wei

The Uetsufumi

Wakabayashi-ke Koki

The Miyashita Documents (also known as The Fuji Documents)

Amatsu-Tatara Hifumi

Saga of Joukan Tomi of Izumo (oral history found in several records)

Shaku Nihongi

Kamiyo Moji (also known as Jindai Moji)

Futomani

Kotodama

Hitsuki Shinji

Mikasafumi

Engishiki

Ame-naru-Fumi (supposedly one of the sacred possessions held by the imperial family)

None of the originals of these records have survived. Therefore, what is available are copies or copies of copies at best. Thus, there are admittedly questions about the authenticity of these records. For these reasons, and more, historians and scholars are understandably nervous about including them in the conversation. While there is merit to being cautious about what textual evidence is or is not dependable, scholars should also not, on the other end of the spectrum, dismiss potential sources of information so carelessly. If the basis for eliminating textual evidence is simply that it is not an original copy, or that there are questions about authenticity that need to be investigated, then there are a lot of conclusions about ancient civilizations and history that must be thrown out immediately because those assumptions have been made on the back of records that are nothing more than oral traditions, for example, recorded hundreds, if not thousands, of years after the supposed events for which they refer. If the sagas of the Vikings, the books of the *Bible*, the Sumerian clay tablets, and other such records are to be accepted as near fact, then a more open mind is needed when working with other ancient manuscripts. Or at least an open mind to investigate the validity of a record first instead of casting it out from scholarly hypocrisy. The supposed legends, myths, and early histories of Japan were likely not even written down from what was originally a set of oral traditions after the adoption of Chinese script beginning in about the sixth century CE. Therefore, there would be obvious flaws, blatant and accidental changes, and misinterpretations of those original histories. Nevertheless, and just as scholars do with the mythologies of other cultures, those stories can be used to glean at least some fraction of truth.

These ancient Japanese texts, along with many others, open up a wide range of avenues of things to study about not just the possible relationship with the islands of Japan in the ancient past and ancient Israel, but they also suggest challenges for other accepted histories and truths about early Chinese as well as Central, North, and

West Asian narratives – alternative narratives that need to be investigated. Some of these tales or records, such as *Hotsuma Tsutaye*, suggest challenges to such things as the long held accepted gender of the goddess Amaterasu, and suggest that as a result of all the numerous copies and translations of the past several hundred years, Amaterasu was not female, and that the original version of the narrative identifies the deity as male. This new interpretation, of course, not only dramatically alters the entire Japanese origin story, but actually brings it more in line with that of the book of Genesis. Others introduce the idea that not only did some of the Lost Tribes of Israel make their way to Japan, but that the connection did not end with that migration – that there continued to be contact between these people well after. Admittedly, those that choose to look deeper into these texts will find that these possible alternative histories introduce controversy into the conversation. Nevertheless, just because controversy is stirred up does not immediately mean that something is not true or does not accurately shed light on the truth.

Again, it can only be hoped that scholars will begin to take these often-ignored records more seriously, and, at the very least, investigate them thoroughly enough to decide more conclusively which can be helpful, and/or what information contained therein can further the dialogue on this and other historical topics related to ancient Asia.

Afterward
Further Considerations

Possibly the most important consideration is the reality that what Shintoism and Judaism were characteristically in ancient days would be unrecognizable to any common observer today. The simple fact is that like any other set of traditions, all collective beliefs, along with their manifested trappings, evolve and change over time; shaped constantly by the very believers themselves and or the circumstances and conditions over the ages. It is true that Shintoism as a formal, organized belief system did not truly begin to emerge until after Buddhism – in the form of the Mahayana tradition – began gaining traction in Japan. It could even be argued that the process of formalizing Shintoism was more of a direct response to, and mechanism for survival and competition against, Buddhism. One might claim further that what is understood today as Shintoism is, in reality, nothing more than a syncretized form with Buddhism, and can no longer be understood to be a separate or stand-alone faith, which is why the two faiths are commonly referred to by Japanese as a hybrid faith, or Shinbutsu-shuugou.

The same could also be said of the evolution Judaism took from its early Semitic form of animism of the Canaanites, Arameans, and other peoples of that region, and the more formalized form it eventually began taking first with Abraham, later during the Exodus from Egypt at the supposed time of Moses, and eventually after the Babylonian Exile, for example. One could even go as far as to argue that, if the accounts outlined in the *Old Testament* are to be believed, Judaism did not begin to take on an institutionalized form until the period of supposed enslavement in Egypt, and, therefore, Egyptian religious practices had the most significant long-lasting impact on the evolution of Judaism from a disparate set of animistic traditions into a formal religious tradition. A similar outside influence, Zoroastrianism under the Babylonians, played a similar part later. Like all faiths, Judaism and Shintoism are merely syncretic combinations of still further collections of other belief systems or traditions.

There is a fairly tricky question that must be raised when dealing with spiritual traditions that are defined as animistic. That is what should be defined as animism and what is formal religion. For most, formal religion is the institutionalized body of believers of a particular doctrine, whereas animism would be lacking those points. For many in the academic community, animistic traditions are a big gray area. There is no consensus on how to approach animism within the greater conversation of religious systems or spirituality. Some are happily open to including animism and believe it is a category of worship, and while perhaps lacking the institutional nature of the more modern recognizable religions, believe these perspectives still provide a valuable understanding of the contributions made in matters of spirituality by various cultures across time. Others do not yet have a firm opinion on the subject. And still others are diametrically opposed to considering the various forms of animism as part of the body of religions and prefer to lump them together as their own category of study. There is, unfortunately, no right or wrong conclusion. Particularly in the case of Shintoism, there is a spiritual viewpoint that so many believe has animistic origins but was later hybridized and institutionalized enough to take on the appearance of a formal religion.

Even the faithful adherents to the modern notions of Shintoism and Judaism are unable to agree upon what those faiths mean. So, how could anyone accurately define what they were like two thousand years, or even five hundred years ago? We can only rely upon what is observable today. There is no documentary or physical evidence to date that has ever been discovered, no smoking gun, which allows us to say definitively that there was at one point a shared past between Shintoism and Judaism. However, this also means that we cannot say with absolute certainty that there was not. If there is anything that can be learned from this historical study, it is that more of an open mind, one ready to welcome new discoveries and possibilities, is needed, not less of one.

Glossary

A

ainu – one of a couple of names the indigenous people of Japan refer to themselves, meaning "the people"

aïy-oïuna – name given by the Yakut people of Siberia for their shamans

asa no ha – *kagome* like symbols used in the crests of many ancient Japanese clans and cities

B

bakufu – Japanese term for supreme military commander

Bani-Israel – collective descendants or children of Israel

Bar Mitzvah – Jewish rite of passage ritual and celebration for young men

Bat Mitzvah – Jewish rite of passage ritual and celebration for young women

bris – Jewish ritualistic circumcision of infant boys on their eighth day of life (*brit milah*)

brit banot – ceremony for infant girls on the eighth day of life

I

brit milah – Jewish ritualistic circumcision of infant boys on their eighth day of life (*bris*)

burakumin – Japanese derogatory term meaning hamlet people (*eta hinin*)

C

chattah – things forbidden or taboo under Jewish law or teachings

cohen – term for Jewish priests (*cohenim* plural)

D

-

E

elohim- Hebrew-Aramaic term for gods

ema – wood plate-like object with the image of a horse

ephod – rectangular cloth tunic worn by a Jewish priest over the robe

Eretz Israel – Hebrew term that refers to the collective homeland of the Jews as supposedly set aside for the faithful by God.

eta hinin – Japanese term meaning filthy non-human

F

-

G

gekkei-goya – a hut like building in which women in early Japan would stay in order to separate themselves from a community during their menstruation cycle

Genpukushiki – Shinto rite of passage ritual or ceremony for young men

guji – high priest in Shintoism

H

haiden – the Holy Place, oratory, the first part of the most sacred building(s) of a Shinto shrine complex

hallah – customary Jewish yeast-leavened bread

hashira – the specific name of the spirits believed to possess the *Oniyabashira-sai* logs

heiden – the barrier in a Shinto shrine that separates the sacred interior from the courtyard, at which common visitors recite prayer

hiragana – one of two syllabic alphabets used by Japanese, now paired with Chinese characters

honden – the most sacred part of the building(s) of a Shinto shrine complex, the Holy of Holies

hoo – bird like figure made of gold on *omikoshi*

horagai – a seashell *yamabushi* use in rituals (*shofar*)

I

inao – the Ainu term for the same religious object known in Japanese as *oonusa* or *oharagushi*

inari – the animal or animal-like representation of a kami, something akin to a totem

J

jichinsai – a ceremonial blessing of a new building or home with the purpose of purifying

jinja – Shinto shrine (*miya* or *yashiro*)

juugyoya – Shinto Feast of Booths

K

kafan – a type of rectangular garment fringed with chords worn by the people of the early Pathan culture

kagome – six-cornered star symbol found to be incorporated at many Shinto shrines

kamui – the Ainu term for a deity

Kamui kotan – the Ainu term for a heaven like existence after death, meaning "place of God"

kanka – ritual practiced by Ryukyu islanders of smearing the blood of a first-born cow about the threshold of the home the evening on the last day of the year (*shimakusarashi)*, meaning "to be overlooked"

kanname-sai – Shinto festivals of first fruits

katakana – one of two syllabic alphabets used by Japanese, now used for spelling foreign words or place-names

kazuki – ceremonial shawl or covering worn by brides during a Shinto wedding

kegare – pollution of a person's soul

kekkonshiki – Shinto wedding ceremony

komainu – lion like creatures in stature form that guard the entrance to the holiest buildings of a Shinto shrine

kosher – fit or allowed to be eaten or used, according to the dietary or ceremonial laws *koyane* – supposedly Japanese term for upper gods

kusanagi no tsurugi – a supposedly sword like object sacred in Shintoism and Japanese royal family

L

laver – the ceremonial washbasin in the Jewish Tabernacle, or later, temples

M

matzah – Jewish unleavened cakes made of grain

matsuri – Shinto priests officiate various important religious ceremonies in which entire communities are expected to participate

miisakuchi – ritual sacrifice made of deer as part of the Ontousai festival

mikveh – Jewish ceremonial bathhouse for the purpose of ritualistic cleansing

misogi – a practice in which water is used to metaphorically washing impurities from a person's soul

mitzvah – Jewish ritual, ceremony, celebration

miya – Japanese shrine (*jinja* or *yashiro*)

mizura – ancient Japanese custom of wearing curled side locks of hair in front of the ears (*peyot*)

mochi – Japanese cake balls made of pounded steamed rice

mohel – male officiate of a bris

mohelet – female officiate of a bris

N

nagashibina – dolls or paper shaped to look like a person used as effigies in Shinto rituals

naorai – sacrificial offerings made of food to the *kami*

natsu matsuri – Shinto Summer Festival (similar to the Jewish Passover festivities)

nebiim – mystic hermit of ancient Western Asia

Nichiyu Dousoron – the Japanese term for the Japanese-Jewish Common Ancestry Theory

ninja – a term that has come to be used to refer to mercenary like groups of warriors from several mountainous regions of central Japan

norito – a prayer recited on behalf of the faithful to a *kami*

O

oharagushi - a bundle of white paper strapped to a bamboo pole made to look like a sheaf of wheat (*ounusa*)

omikoshi – the portable Shinto shrine that is part of nearly all Shinto festivals

oniya bashira – Shinto sacrifice pilar part of the rituals involved in the *Ontousai* festival

onsen – Japanese community bathhouse

ooharai – a term referring to ceremonies or rituals of Shintoism

osechi ryori – traditional foods consumed by Japanese during the first three days of the New Year

oshichiya – a naming ceremony performed in early Japan on the eighth day of a child's life

osouji – the practice at New Years in Japan of people cleaning their homes thoroughly and disposing of unneeded things in order to ritualistically cleanse their home for the New Year

ounusa – a bundle of white paper strapped to a bamboo pole made to look like a sheaf of wheat (*oharagushi*)

P

peyot – the side curls of hair worn by Jewish men. It is more characteristically worn now by Jewish men of more conservative leanings (*mizura*)

Q

-

R

roro-oshiraya – the ritualistic cleansing women in early Japan underwent when the menstruation cycle had ended and before rejoining their community

S

saishi – Shinto rituals (*ooharai*)

sake – rice wine

Samai – one of the name the Ainu give their people

Samoro – name the Ainu use for their land, the land others know as Japan

samurai – the warrior class of ancient early Japanese society, meaning "one/those that serves"

shaba umpe – a phylactery-like object worn around the crown or forward of the head by Ainu chieftains or other such high officials on special religious occasions

shabbath – Hebrew term for sabbath

shalom zakhar – celebratory feast after a *bris*

shamusho – administrative building at Shinto shrines

shamashut – administrative buildings at Jewish synagogues

shiki – the Japanese term for document of manuscript

shimakusarashi – ritual practiced by Ryukyu islanders of smearing the blood of a first-born cow about the threshold of the home the evening on the last day of the year (*kanka)*, meaning "to cast away"

Shin-Butsu shuugou – the Japanese term that refers to the amalgamation of Shinto and Buddhism as a syncretic faith

shinshoku – term for a Shinto priest

shinzen kekkon – Shinto wedding ceremony

shofar – the rams horn used by Jewish priests

shougun – Japanese title for supreme military commanders

sib – the Hebrew-Aramaic term for a cohort of priests

Sinim – Hebrew term for the area of China

sumo – Japanese traditional wrestling

T

taika- means "hope" in early Japanese

taiko – drums first used for Shinto ceremonies

tefillin- the phylactery object worn at the forehead by Jewish priests

Teinei-pokua-shiri – the Ainu term for a hell-like existence after death

temizuya – the ceremonial washbasins found at Shinto shrines

tengu – a Japanese mythological creature or spirit the mountains

tikva – means "hope" in Hebrew-Aramaic

tokin – the phylactery object worn at the forehead by Shinto priests and *yamabushi* monks

tora no maki – scroll of the tora

torii – gateways of Shinto shrines

tsumi – a taboo or something forbidden

tzitzit – the rectangular outer garment fringed with chords and worn by Jewish priests

U

uji – Japanese term for lineage group of clan

utagaki – singing and dancing that accompanies Shinto festivals

utari – one of a couple of names the indigenous people of Japan use to refer to themselves

V

-

W

-

X

-

Y

Yahweh – the less honorific name of many of the ancient Semitic peoples of Western Asia, including the Canaanites

yamabushi – Shinto mountain hermit monks

yasaka no magatama – a supposedly crystal-like object that is sacred in Shintoism and Japanese royal family

yashiro – Shinto shrine (*miya* or *jinja*)

yata no kagami – a supposedly mirror-like object that is considered sacred in Shintoism and the Japanese royal family

yukara – Ainu folktales

-

References

"5 Uniquely Japanese Events in a Child's First Year." *Savvy Tokyo*, 13 Jan. 2022, https://savvytokyo.com/five-uniquely-japanese-events-childs-first-year/.

"According to the Customs of Moses and Shinto." *YouTube*, YouTube, 16 Dec. 2020, https://www.youtube.com/watch?v=4tJ1fIvsFHA. Accessed 16 Dec. 2022.

Alvarez, Carla. "What's the Name of Your Golden Calf?" *Raised to Walk*, 3 June 2021, http://raisedtowalk.org/the-walk/whats-the-name-of-your-golden-calf/.

"Amishav USA." *Kulanu.org*, https://kulanu.org/wp-content/uploads/magazines/1993-winter.pdf.

"Ancient Egypt Apis Bull: Apis the Bull God: Golden Calf: Divine Bull Cults." *Facts About Ancient Egyptians*, https://ancientegyptianfacts.com/ancient-egypt-apis-bull.html.

Anonymous. "Japanese Emperor Begins Last Accession Rite: Spending the Night with a Goddess." *NDTV.com*, 14 Nov. 2019, https://www.ndtv.com/world-news/japanese-emperor-begins-last-major-accession-rite-spending-night-with-goddess-2132556.

"Assyrian Bracelet." *World History Encyclopedia*, https://www.worldhistory.org/image/4073/assyrian-bracelet/.

Aston, W. G. *Nihongi: Chronicles of Japan from the Earliest Times to A.D. 697*. Cossimo Classics, 2008.

Avichail, Eliyahu. *The Tribes of Israel: The Lost and the Dispersed*. Amishav, 2013.

Batchelor, John. *Specimens of Ainu Folk-Lore*. Tokyo, Japan. 1888-1893.

"bur Study: The Wave Offering & Jesus." *Southlawn Church of God*, http://www.southlawncog.org/bible-study-the-wave-offering--jesus.html.

Blaker, Cameron. *The Catalpa Bow: A Study of Shamanistic Practices in Japan*. Routledge Publishing, London UK. 1999.

Bock, Felicia. *Engi-Shiki: Ceremonial Procedures of the Engi Era*. 1970. Tokyo, JP, Sophia University, 1966.

Bodart-Bailey, Beatrice M. *Furthest Goal: Engelbert Kaempfer's Encounter with Tokugawa Japan*. Routledge, 2016.

"Book of Exodus." *Wikimedia Commons*, Wikimedia Foundation, Inc., 10 May 2019, https://commons.wikimedia.org/wiki/Book_of_Exodus.

Cali, Joseph. "Shinto Shrines of Japan.," 1 Jan. 1970, http://shintoshrinesofjapanblogguide.blogspot.com/2013/04/excerpts-from-shinto-shrines-guide-to.html.

"Canaanite Religion." *Wikipedia*, Wikimedia Foundation, 7 May 2022, https://en.wikipedia.org/wiki/Canaanite_religion.

Ceremonial Wrestlers, Jars on Heads, Struggle in Bronze, https://www.goldenageproject.org.uk/482.php.

Chamberlain, Basi Hall. *Aino Folk-tales*. London, UK, 1888.

Como, Michael. *Weaving and Binding: Immigrant Gods and Female Immortals in Ancient Japan.* Honolulu, University of Hawaii Press, 2010.

Eidelberg, Joseph. *The Japanese and the Ten Lost Tribes of Israel.* Gefen Publishing House, 2014.

Eidelberg, Joseph. *The Biblical Hebrew Origin of the Japanese People.* Gefen Publishing House, 2005.

"Experience the Tabernacle: An Interview with Jeanne Whittaker." Bible Gateway Blog, 31 Jan. 2020, https://www.biblegateway.com/blog/2014/07/experience-the-tabernacle-an-interview-with-jeanne-whittaker/.

Fedorchuk, Artem. "Jewish Cemeteries of the Crimea: History of Research and Present State of Affairs." *Jews of Eurasia*, http://jewseurasia.org/page34/news23519.html.

"From Prejudice to Pride." *Hakai Magazine*, hakaimagazine.com/features/prejudice-pride/.

"Fukuchiyama, Kyoto." *Wikiwand*, https://www.wikiwand.com/en/Fukuchiyama,_Kyoto.

Gilad, Elon. "When the Jews Believed in Other Gods." *Haaretz.com*, Haaretz, 26 July 2018, https://www.haaretz.com/archaeology/2018-07-26/ty-article-magazine/.premium/when-the-jews-believed-in-other-gods/0000017f-dc52-d856-a37f-fdd222920000.

Guénon René, and S. D. Fohr. *The King of the World.* Sophia Perennis, 2004.

Gunnarsdóttir, Ellen Dröfn, et al. "Larger Mitochondrial DNA than Y-Chromosome Differences between Matrilocal and Patrilocal Groups from Sumatra." *Nature News*, Nature Publishing Group, 8 Mar. 2011, https://www.nature.com/articles/ncomms1235.

"Haplogroup." *Wikipedia*, Wikimedia Foundation, 8 May

2022, https://en.wikipedia.org/wiki/Haplogroup.

"Harai." *Encyclopædia Britannica, Inc.*, https://www.britannica.com/topic/harai.

Hayashi, Hiroshi, director. *The Lost Ten Tribes of Israel + Japan. YouTube*, YouTube, 10 July 2019, https://www.youtube.com/watch?v=A493nqP6HqM. Accessed 10 Jan. 2023.

Hays, Jeffrey. "Ainu: Their History, Art, Life, Rituals, Clothes and Bears | Facts and Details." https://factsanddetails.com, factsanddetails.com/japan/cat18/sub119/item638.html.

Hays, Jeffrey. "Shinto Shrines, Priests, Rituals and Customs." https://factsanddetails.com/japan/cat16/sub182/item590.html.

Heiser, Michael S., et al. "Why the Ark of the Covenant Will Never Be Found." *Word by Word*, 26 Apr. 2022, https://www.logos.com/grow/ark-covenant-will-never-found/.

Hitchcock, Romyn. *The Ainos of Yezo*. U.S. National Museum, 1890.

Hodge, Bodie, and Roger Todd Patterson. *World Religions and Cults*. Master Books, 2016.

"Holy of Holies." *Wikiwand*, https://www.wikiwand.com/en/Holy_of_Holies.

I24News. *Arimasa Kubo on the Shinto Religion and Judaism. YouTube*, YouTube, 12 Apr. 2021, https://www.youtube.com/watch?v=RrXtrHwynrY. Accessed 16 Dec. 2022.

I24News. *Japan and the Lost Tribes. YouTube*, YouTube, 12 Apr. 2021, https://www.youtube.com/watch?v=Y-xF4lLK1PE. Accessed 16 Dec. 2022.

"Israel's Exodus from Egypt and Entry into Canaan." *The Church of Jesus Christ of Latter-Day Saints*, https://www.churchofjesuschrist.org/study/scriptures/bible-maps/map-2?lang=eng.

"Is the Ark of the Covenant Really in Ethiopia?" *Yesterday's Articles | Yesterday Channel, UKTV Play*, 22 Feb. 2016, https://yesterday.uktv.co.uk/blogs/article/ark-covenant-really-ethiopia/.

"Japanese & Hebrew Similarities – Sacred Structures." *Thechristianbushido*, 2 Nov. 2020, https://thechristianbushido.wordpress.com/japanese-hebrew-similarities-sacred-structures/.

"Japanese Author Traces Nippon Origin to Hebrew Race." *Jewish Telegraphic Agency*, 20 Mar. 2015, https://www.jta.org/archive/japanese-author-traces-nippon-origin-to-hebrew-race.

"Jesus and the Brazen Laver." *Grace and Truth*, 16 July 2015, https://graceandtruth.me/2015/07/16/jesus-and-the-brazen-laver/.

"Kamakura's Hanzobo Shrine - Kamakura, Kanagawa." *JapanTravel*, https://en.japantravel.com/kanagawa/kamakura-s-hanzobo-shrine/21453.

"Kabayama Site." *Wikipedia, Wikimedia Foundation*, 13 May 2020, https://en.wikipedia.org/wiki/Kabayama_Site.

Kasulis, Thomas P. *Shinto: The Way Home*. University of Hawaii Press, 2004.

Kawanua, Nocturnal, director. *The Roots of Japan Were Ancient Israel!? YouTube*, YouTube, 21 Aug. 2011, https://www.youtube.com/watch?v=TLc30VSPdgY. Accessed 10 Jan. 2023.

"Komainu." *Wikipedia*, Wikimedia Foundation, 24 Nov. 2021, https://en.wikipedia.org/wiki/Komainu.

Kowner, Rotem, «'Lighter than Yellow, but Not Enough': Western Discourse on the Japanese 'Race', 1854–1904». *The Historical Journal*, 43 (1): 103–131, 2000.

Kubo, Arimasa. "DNA Shows Japanese and Jewish Peoples Are Relatives," https://remnant-p.com/japjewdna.htm.

Kubo, Arimasa. "Israelites Came to Ancient Japan." *Journal of Religion and Psychical Research*, vol. 22, no. 3, July 1999, pp. 134–158.

Kubo, Arimasa. *Suwa-Taisha Shrine and the Lost Tribes of Israel*. https://mas-eng.com/SuwaIsraelites.htm.

Kuroita, Katsumi. *Nihon Shoki*. Yoshikawa Kōbunkan, 2007.

Lee, Samuel. *Rediscovering Japan, Reintroducing Christendom: Two Thousand Years of Christian History in Japan*. Hamilton Books, 2010.

Linsley, Alice C. "Solving the Ainu Mystery." *Just Genesis*, 29 Dec. 2014, http://jandyongenesis.blogspot.com/2014/12/solving-ainu-mystery.html.

"Lost Tribes of Israel | Where Are the Ten Lost Tribes?" *Public Broadcasting Service*, https://www.pbs.org/wgbh/nova/israel/losttribes3.html.

Manda, Gensen, et al. *Shinsen Shōjiroku*. Shintō Taikei Hensankai, 1981.

Markey, Dell, and Lewis Loflin. "The Babylonian Exile and the Jewish Religion.," http://www.jewishwikipedia.info/movement_babylon.html.

Marett, R.R.. *Aboriginal Siberia: A Study in Social Anthropology*. Oxford Press, 1914.

Mauldin, Leon. "Herod's Gate/Flower Gate." *Leon's Message Board*, 9 July 2011, https://leonmauldin. blog/2011/07/08/herods-gateflower-gate/.

McLeod, Nicholas. *Epitome of the Ancient History of Japan*. Rising Sun, 1878.

Medzini, M. *Under the Shadow of the Rising Sun: Japan and the Jews During the Holocaust Era*. Academic Studies Press, 2016.

"Mikoshi and Ark / Shinto and Judaism / Yahweh in Geku.," 5 Feb. 2020, https://yamatopeople.blogspot.com/2016/11/ mikoshi-and-ark-shinto-and-judaism.html.

Miura, James. "Not Even Human: The Birth of the Outcaste in Tokugawa Japan." *Hohonu*, vol. 17, 2019, https:// doi.org/https://hilo.hawaii.edu/campuscenter/hohonu/ volumes/documents/NotEvenHumanTheBirthoftheOut-casteinTokugawaJapan.pdf.

Miura, Kiyoko. *Yukara Epos of the Ainus: Study and Translation of Kamuy-Yukara*. 2015. https://www.sacred-texts. com/shi/ainu/yukara.htm

Morris-Suzuki, Tessa. "Indigenous Diplomacy: Sakhalin Ainu (Enchiw) in the Shaping of Modern East Asia (Part 2: Voices and Silences)." *The Asia-Pacific Journal*, vol. 18, no. 23, ser. 5, 1 Dec. 2020. 5, https://doi.org/https://apjjf. org/2020/23/Morris-Suzuki.html.

"Mt Karkom." *BibleWalks 500+ Sites*, 22 May 2021, https://www.biblewalks.com/karkom.

Neusner, Jacob, and Alan J Avery-Peck. *The Blackwell Companion to Judaism*. Malden, Ma, Blackwell Publishing, 2003.

Nishinomiya City [Hyōgo Prefecture - Japan], https:// www.crwflags.com/fotw/flags/jp-28-ni.html.

Odlum, Edward Faraday. *Who Are the Japanese?* Covenant Publishing Co., 1933.

Ō Yasumaro, and Kazutami Nishimiya. *Kojiki.* Shinchōsha, 2014.

"Ōmuta, Fukuoka." *Wikiwand,* https://www.wikiwand.com/en/%C5%8Cmuta,_Fukuoka.

"Ōnusa." *Wikipedia, Wikimedia Foundation,* 6 May 2022, https://en.wikipedia.org/wiki/%C5%8Cnusa.

Parfitt, Tudor. *The Lost Tribes of Israel: The History of a Myth.* Weidenfeld & Nicolson, Ltd., 2002.

Perrin, Jonathon. "'Shofar Away': An Akhenaten Connection to the Jewish New Year." *Ancient Origins,* 8 Nov. 2019, https://www.ancient-origins.net/history-ancient-traditions/shofar-0012833.

Peterson, Benjamin, and Yukie Chiri. *The Song the Owl God Sang: The Collected Ainu Legends of Chiri Yukie.* BJS Books, 2013.

Kojiki. Translated by Donald L. Philippi, Princeton, NJ, Princeton University Pres, 2015.

Philippi, Donald L. *Norito: A Translation of the Ancient Japanese Ritual Prayers.* Princeton Univ. Press, 1990.

Philippi, Donald L., and Gary Snyder. *Songs of Gods, Songs of Humans: The Epic Tradition of the Ainu.* Princeton University Press, 2015.

"Phylactery Definition & Meaning." *Merriam-Webster,* https://www.merriam-webster.com/dictionary/phylactery.

Plant, Thomas W. *The Japanese - Who Are They?* Destiny Publishers, 1938.

"Pin on Japanese Inspired." *Pinterest,* 14 July 2013, https://

www.pinterest.com/pin/502432902149251328/.

"Ritual Practices and Institutions." *Encyclopædia Britannica, Inc.*, https://www.britannica.com/topic/Shinto/Ritual-practices-and-institutions.

Satow, Ernist, and Karl Florenz. *Ancient Japanese Rituals.* London, UK, Routledge, 16 July 2014.

"Sca Japanese Inspiration." *Pinterest*, 8 Oct. 2017, https://www.pinterest.com/pin/527132331376628219/.

Shachan, Avigdor, et al. *In the Footsteps of the Lost Ten Tribes*. Kobe Peace Research Institute, 2013.

Shillony, Ben-Ami. *The Jews and Japanese: The Successful Outsiders*. Tuttle, 1992.

"Shinto Worship." *BBC*, 16 Sept. 2009, https://www.bbc.co.uk/religion/religions/shinto/ritesrituals/worship_1.shtml.

Siddle, Richard. *Race, Resistance, and the Ainu of Japan*. Routledge, 1996.

Smith, Alice Elsa. "Comparative Study of Judaism and Shinto." *University of the Pacific Scholarly Commons*, June 1949, https://doi.org/https://scholarlycommons.pacific.edu/uop_etds.

Stephen Tam. "The Golden Garments." *Solomon's Temple*, http://www.3dbibleproject.com/en/temple/study/gold_garments.htm?study=on.

Sweeney, Marvin A. "The Rights and Duties of Kingship in Israel" *Rights and Duties of Kingship in Israel*, 16 May 2022, https://www.bibleodyssey.org/en/passages/related-articles/rights-and-duties-of-kingship-in-israel.

Tajima, Atsushi, and Masayori Hayami, et. al. "Genetic Origins of the Ainu Inferred from Combined DNA Analyses of Maternal and Paternal Lineages." *Journal of Hu-*

man Genetics, no. 49, 1 Apr. 2004, pp. 187–193., https://doi.org/https://www.nature.com/articles/jhg200432.

Takaya Shrine: Superb Views of the Torii in the Sky. https://matcha-jp.com/en/11031.

Taronas, Laura. "Akhenaten: The Mysteries of Religious Revolution." *ARCE*, https://www.arce.org/resource/akhenaten-mysteries-religious-revolution#:~:text=Akhenaten%20came%20to%20power%20as,that%20centered%20on%20the%20Aten.

"Temizuya: The Cleansing Ritual." *Nippon.com*, 30 May 2020, https://www.nippon.com/en/views/b05205/.

"Temple Mount." *BiblePlaces.com*, 7 Oct. 2021, https://www.bibleplaces.com/templemount/.

Teshima Ikurō. *The Ancient Jewish Diaspora in Japan: The Tribe of Hada, Their Religious and Cultural Influence.* Makuya Tokyo Bible Seminary, 1976.

"The Ainu, Indigenous People of Japan, Facing the Challenges of Identity Reconstruction." *www.gis-reseau-asie.org*, www.gis-reseau-asie.org/en/ainu-indigenous-people-japan-facing-challenges-identity-reconstruction.

"The Brit Milah (BRIS): What You Need to Know." *My Jewish Learning*, 6 May 2022, https://www.myjewishlearning.com/article/the-brit-milah-bris-ceremony/.

The Modern Alchemist, 14 Aug. 2020, https://didanawisgi.tumblr.com/post/626461990525796352/japan-the-kagome-crest-can-be-found-in-some-of.

"The Unusual Sacred Artifacts That King Solomon Possessed." *Monkey Elf | Aliens, Angels and the Apocalypse*, 2 Aug. 2020, https://www.monkeyandelf.com/the-unusual-sacred-artifacts-that-king-solomon-possessed/.

"Three-Legged Crow." *Wikipedia*, Wikimedia Foundation, 10 Sept. 2022, https://en.wikipedia.org/wiki/Three-legged_crow.

"Throne of Solomon." *Wikipedia*, Wikimedia Foundation, 11 Apr. 2022, https://en.wikipedia.org/wiki/Throne_of_Solomon.

Ullman, Yirmiyahu. "The Lost Jews the Ten Tribes." *Ohr Somayach*, 24 July 2004, https://ohr.edu/yhiy/article.php/1788.

Ullman, Yirmiyahu. "The Lost Tribes - Will They Return." *Ohr Somayach*, 9 Oct. 2004, https://ohr.edu/explore_judaism/ask_the_rabbi/ask_the_rabbi/1876.

Ullman, Yirmiyahu. "The Lost Tribes Where Are They Today?" *Ohr Somayach*, 28 Aug. 2004, https://ohr.edu/yhiy/article.php/1817.

"Wakkanai." *Wikiwand*, https://www.wikiwand.com/en/Wakkanai.

Weber, Max. *Ancient Judaism*. Free Press, 1967.

World Turtle Media. *The Mystery of Jews in Japan ~ Susanoo-No-Mikoto Part I*. *YouTube*, YouTube, 11 May 2016, https://www.youtube.com/watch?v=2Ae3rnNQqc-M&t=27s. Accessed 16 Dec. 2022.

"Yamabushi Mountain Monks of Yamagata." *The Hidden Japan*, https://www.thehiddenjapan.com/yamabushi.

"Yamabushi Mountain Priests." *Yamabushi Mountain Priests | Japan Experience*, https://www.japan-experience.com/plan-your-trip/to-know/understanding-japan/yamabushi.

Yoshiwara, Roger. *Sumerian and Japanese: A Comparative Language Study*. Japan English Service, 1991.

www.ingramcontent.com/pod-product-compliance
Lightning Source LLC
Chambersburg PA
CBHW011229120626
46549CB00008B/3192